Social Justice

OPPOSING VIEWPOINTS®

Social Justice

OPPOSING VIEWPOINTS®

Other Books of Related Interest

Social Justice

OPPOSING VIEWPOINTS ®

William Dudley, *Book Editor*

Bruce Glassman, *Vice President*
Bonnie Szumski, *Publisher*
Helen Cothran, *Managing Editor*

OPPOSING
VIEWPOINTS®
SERIES

GREENHAVEN PRESS
An imprint of Thomson Gale, a part of The Thomson Corporation

THOMSON
™
GALE

Detroit • New York • San Francisco • San Diego • New Haven, Conn.
Waterville, Maine • London • Munich

6|05

#56942041

© 2005 Thomson Gale, a part of The Thomson Corporation.

Thomson and Star Logo are trademarks and Gale and Greenhaven Press are registered trademarks used herein under license.

For more information, contact
Greenhaven Press
27500 Drake Rd.
Farmington Hills, MI 48331-3535
Or you can visit our Internet site at http://www.gale.com

Cover credit: © Getty Images

LIBRARY OF CONGRESS CATALOGING-IN-PUBLICATION DATA

Social justice : opposing viewpoints / William Dudley, book editor.
    p. cm. — (Opposing viewpoints series)
Includes bibliographical references and index.
ISBN 0-7377-2961-9 (lib. : alk. paper) — ISBN 0-7377-2962-7 (pbk. : alk. paper)
    1. Equality—United States. 2. Social justice—United States. 3. African
Americans—Civil rights. 4. Women's rights—United States. 5. Capitalism—Social
aspects. I. Dudley, William. II. Opposing viewpoints series (Unnumbered)
HN90.S6S56 2005
305'.0973—dc22   2004060626

Printed in the United States of America

"Congress shall make
no law...abridging the
freedom of speech, or of
the press."

First Amendment to the U.S. Constitution

The basic foundation of our democracy is the First
Amendment guarantee of freedom of expression.
The Opposing Viewpoints Series is dedicated to the
concept of this basic freedom and the idea that it is
more important to practice it than to enshrine it.

Contents

Why Consider Opposing Viewpoints?

"The only way in which a human being can make some approach to knowing the whole of a subject is by hearing what can be said about it by persons of every variety of opinion and studying all modes in which it can be looked at by every character of mind. No wise man ever acquired his wisdom in any mode but this."

John Stuart Mill

In our media-intensive culture it is not difficult to find differing opinions. Thousands of newspapers and magazines and dozens of radio and television talk shows resound with differing points of view. The difficulty lies in deciding which opinion to agree with and which "experts" seem the most credible. The more inundated we become with differing opinions and claims, the more essential it is to hone critical reading and thinking skills to evaluate these ideas. Opposing Viewpoints books address this problem directly by presenting stimulating debates that can be used to enhance and teach these skills. The varied opinions contained in each book examine many different aspects of a single issue. While examining these conveniently edited opposing views, readers can develop critical thinking skills such as the ability to compare and contrast authors' credibility, facts, argumentation styles, use of persuasive techniques, and other stylistic tools. In short, the Opposing Viewpoints Series is an ideal way to attain the higher-level thinking and reading skills so essential in a culture of diverse and contradictory opinions.

In addition to providing a tool for critical thinking, Opposing Viewpoints books challenge readers to question their own strongly held opinions and assumptions. Most people form their opinions on the basis of upbringing, peer pressure, and personal, cultural, or professional bias. By reading carefully balanced opposing views, readers must directly confront new ideas as well as the opinions of those with whom they disagree. This is not to simplistically argue that everyone who reads opposing views will—or should—change his or her opinion. Instead, the series enhances readers' understanding of their own views by encouraging confrontation with opposing ideas. Careful examination of others' views can lead to the readers' understanding of the logical inconsistencies in their own opinions, perspective on why they hold an opinion, and the consideration of the possibility that their opinion requires further evaluation.

Evaluating Other Opinions

To ensure that this type of examination occurs, Opposing Viewpoints books present all types of opinions. Prominent spokespeople on different sides of each issue as well as well-known professionals from many disciplines challenge the reader. An additional goal of the series is to provide a forum for other, less known, or even unpopular viewpoints. The opinion of an ordinary person who has had to make the decision to cut off life support from a terminally ill relative, for example, may be just as valuable and provide just as much insight as a medical ethicist's professional opinion. The editors have two additional purposes in including these less known views. One, the editors encourage readers to respect others' opinions—even when not enhanced by professional credibility. It is only by reading or listening to and objectively evaluating others' ideas that one can determine whether they are worthy of consideration. Two, the inclusion of such viewpoints encourages the important critical thinking skill of objectively evaluating an author's credentials and bias. This evaluation will illuminate an author's reasons for taking a particular stance on an issue and will aid in readers' evaluation of the author's ideas.

It is our hope that these books will give readers a deeper understanding of the issues debated and an appreciation of the complexity of even seemingly simple issues when good and honest people disagree. This awareness is particularly important in a democratic society such as ours in which people enter into public debate to determine the common good. Those with whom one disagrees should not be regarded as enemies but rather as people whose views deserve careful examination and may shed light on one's own.

Thomas Jefferson once said that "difference of opinion leads to inquiry, and inquiry to truth." Jefferson, a broadly educated man, argued that "if a nation expects to be ignorant and free . . . it expects what never was and never will be." As individuals and as a nation, it is imperative that we consider the opinions of others and examine them with skill and discernment. The Opposing Viewpoints Series is intended to help readers achieve this goal.

David L. Bender and Bruno Leone,
Founders

Greenhaven Press anthologies primarily consist of previously published material taken from a variety of sources, including periodicals, books, scholarly journals, newspapers, government documents, and position papers from private and public organizations. These original sources are often edited for length and to ensure their accessibility for a young adult audience. The anthology editors also change the original titles of these works in order to clearly present the main thesis of each viewpoint and to explicitly indicate the opinion presented in the viewpoint. These alterations are made in consideration of both the reading and comprehension levels of a young adult audience. Every effort is made to ensure that Greenhaven Press accurately reflects the original intent of the authors included in this anthology.

Introduction

"In its most rudimentary form, social justice can be thought of as the fair distribution of society's benefits and responsibilities. But what does fair distribution mean? What might be perceived as fair to one person or group may not be perceived as fair by another."
—*Patricia McGrath Morris, 2002.*

The meaning of "justice" has been debated by the ancient Greek philosophers Socrates and Plato. The term *social justice* is more recent; it can be traced back to nineteenth-century writings, many of which are from Roman Catholic priests and thinkers such as Antonio Rosmini-Serbati and Luigi Taparelli d'Azeglio, who were responding to the social upheavals and mass urban poverty that accompanied the Industrial Revolution. The religious roots of social justice theory are evident to this day. Catholic bishops and other religious leaders often use the term in their critiques of modern society. Institutions that have "social justice" in their name are as likely as not to be Roman Catholic or other religious organizations working for social change. In a 1997 article, Joe Sullivan, a parish organizer for the Catholic Charities Office for Social Justice in St. Paul, Minnesota, draws on two well-known Bible stories to define what social justice is and to make a distinction between social charity and social justice.

The gospel story of the Good Samaritan is a clear example of social charity. In the story a passing stranger proves himself a "good neighbor" when he rescues a person who has been beaten by robbers (after others had passed the victim by). The hero of the story does not "attempt to survey the causes of highway banditry," writes Sullivan, but instead "provides temporary and immediate relief to someone in need." His actions thus qualify as social charity, which Sullivan defines as acts by individuals and small groups to provide for immediate needs through direct services such as food and shelter. These services—such as homeless shelters, food pantries, and emergency aid campaigns—treat the *effects* of injustice and are usually not controversial.

The biblical Exodus story, on the other hand, provides an example of social justice. It describes how Moses led the Hebrews out of slavery in Egypt. Moses did not ask Egypt's ruler for better food and medicine for the slaves, which would have been an act of charity. Instead, he demanded that Egyptian society be changed so that the Hebrews would no longer be enslaved. His actions, Sullivan argues, qualify as social justice, which he defines as collective public acts that respond to long-term needs, promote social change in institutions, and are directed at *root causes* rather than symptoms of injustice. He notes that actions promoting social justice, such as community organizing and legislative advocacy are, unlike social charity activities, often controversial.

A contemporary example illustrating the difference between social charity and social justice involves urban poverty. Catholic and other religious charities often run homeless shelters and other services for poor families and individuals. But in addition to such charity work, religious leaders have turned to political activism in an attempt to answer the question of why people cannot afford housing. Some religious activists have concluded that one answer is that the jobs people can find do not pay enough; these activists thus press city and county governments to institute "living wage" rules mandating that governments and city contractors pay wages that allow workers to escape poverty. As is often the case with policies aimed at promoting social justice, living wage ordinances have proven controversial. For example, policy analyst Carl F. Horowitz is among those who have criticized such laws and the theories behind them. The idea that the "lowest-paid workers are victims of social injustice rectifiable through aggressive political action" is wrong, he asserts; they instead "suffer from a lack of skills."

The primary reason that social justice activities engender controversy while acts of charity do not is because actions to promote social justice challenge the status quo. Dom Helder Camara, a Roman Catholic bishop from Brazil, once stated, "When I gave food to the poor, they called me a saint. When I asked why the poor had no food, they called me a communist." Social justice initiatives, unlike works of charity, tend to raise questions about how society is arranged and whether people who are not poor owe something to those who are. Such questions may be unsettling to those who are well-off and who want to believe that their good fortune is the product of their own hard work and abilities and not a result of discrimination or other unjust social arrangements.

The authors in *Opposing Viewpoints: Social Justice* examine several controversies surrounding social justice as they debate the following questions: Should America Do More to Reduce Economic Inequality? What Policies Would Promote Social Justice for African Americans? What Policies Would Promote Social Justice for Women? Is Global Social Justice Being Upheld? These articles cover a wide array of issues, but all of them address to some extent the question of what should be done—beyond charity—to attain justice for all members of society.

CHAPTER 1

Should America Do More to Reduce Economic Inequality?

Chapter Preface

In 1979 the Congressional Budget Office (CBO) began to collect data comparing income trends of Americans at different economic levels. The data collected since then suggests that the gap between the rich elite and the poor and middle class is growing. In 1979 the average annual income (after taxes) of someone in the poorest 40 percentile was $18,695. Twenty-one years later, in 2000, that number had risen to $21,118. However, during that same time period, the after-tax income of the wealthiest 1 percent of Americans more than tripled, from $286,300 to $862,700 (figures have been adjusted for inflation). In 1979 the total after-tax income of the wealthiest 1 percent of Americans was less than half the total income of the bottom 40 percent; by 2000 the income of the wealthiest 1 percent had exceeded that of the poorest 40 percent of Americans.

Disagreements exist as to whether an increase in economic equality is a problem that must be solved by higher taxes on the wealthy or by other government actions. Some maintain that inequality is an inevitable and necessary component of America's free-market economy—a system they believe has made this nation a "land of opportunity" for those who work hard and have talent and good ideas. Economist Isabel V. Sawhill contends that "inequality reflects differences in individual talent and effort, and as such is a spur to higher economic growth, as well as just compensation for unequal effort and skill." She concludes that income inequality "is the price we pay for a dynamic economy." Like Sawhill, many Americans do not necessarily view income inequality as a problem. American attitudes toward inequality are shaped by the belief that those at the bottom can successfully work their way to the top—and that all Americans have a roughly equal opportunity to succeed on their own merits. "People accept inequality," asserts Purdue University sociologist Robert Perrucci, "if they think there is opportunity."

However, others argue that income inequality among families may create inequality of opportunity as well. Economist Michael D. Yates, in his book *Naming the System: Inequality and Work in the Global System*, asks readers to compare the lives of a child born to a high-income family in a fashionable neighborhood and another child raised by a single mom in an impoverished, crime-ridden ghetto. "Which mother will have the best health care? . . . Which child is more likely to get adequate nutrition and have good health care in early childhood? If the poor child does not have these things, who will return to this child the brain cells lost as a consequence? . . . Which child will go to the better school? Which will have access to books . . . and computers in the home?" Yates concludes that the United States must do more to equalize opportunities for its children.

As the Congressional Budget Office data suggest, the growing gap between rich and poor is real. The debate now is what to do about the gap, if anything. The viewpoints in this chapter present various views on economic inequality in the United States and what social policies can best address it.

> *"Astonishing as it seems, no one in official Washington seems embarrassed by the fact that the gap between rich and poor is greater than it's been in 50 years."*

Economic Inequality Is a Serious Problem in America

Bill Moyers

Bill Moyers is a television journalist, author, and social commentator. He also served as press secretary under President Lyndon Johnson. In the following viewpoint, excerpted from a 2004 speech, he argues that the gap between the rich and poor in the United States is large and growing to such an extent as to call into question the fundamental fairness of American society. He further contends that the wealthy in America have had increasing success in "rigging" the American political system for their own benefit. At the same time, Moyers claims, poor and middle-class Americans are working longer hours, experiencing greater economic insecurity, and wielding less political clout than in previous generations.

As you read, consider the following questions:
1. What two families does Moyers describe?
2. What does equality mean, besides equal incomes, according to the author?
3. What forces and people are threatening equality in America, according to Moyers?

Bill Moyers, keynote address at the Inequality Matters Forum, New York University, June 3, 2004. Copyright © 2004 by Bill Moyers. Reproduced by permission.

Nothing seems to embarrass the political class in Washington today. Not the fact that more children are growing up in poverty in America than in any other industrial nation; not the fact that millions of workers are actually making less money today in real dollars than they did twenty years ago; not the fact that working people are putting in longer and longer hours and still falling behind; not the fact that while we have the most advanced medical care in the world, nearly 44 million Americans—eight out of ten of them in working families—are uninsured and cannot get the basic care they need.

Astonishing as it seems, no one in official Washington seems embarrassed by the fact that the gap between rich and poor is greater than it's been in 50 years—the worst inequality among all Western nations. Or that we are experiencing a shift in poverty. For years it was said those people down there at the bottom were single, jobless mothers. For years they were told work, education, and marriage is how they move up the economic ladder. But poverty is showing up where we didn't expect it—among families that include two parents, a worker, and a head of the household with more than a high school education. These are the newly poor. Our political, financial and business class expects them to climb out of poverty on an escalator moving downward.

Two Families

Let me tell you about the Stanleys and the Neumanns. During the last decade, I produced a series of documentaries for PBS [the Public Broadcasting System] called "Surviving the Good Times." The title refers to the boom time of the '90s when the country achieved the longest period of economic growth in its entire history. Some good things happened then, but not everyone shared equally in the benefits. To the contrary. The decade began with a sustained period of downsizing by corporations moving jobs out of America, and many of those people never recovered what was taken from them. We decided early on to tell the stories of two families in Milwaukee—one black, one white—whose breadwinners were laid off in the first wave of layoffs in 1991. We reported on how they were coping with the wrenching changes in their lives, and we stayed with them over the next ten years as they tried to find a place in the new global economy. They're the kind of Americans my mother would have called "the salt of the earth." They love their kids, care about their communities, go to church every Sunday, and work hard all week—both mothers have had to take full-time jobs.

During our time with them, the fathers in both families became seriously ill. One had to stay in the hospital two months, putting his family $30,000 in debt because they didn't have adequate health insurance. We were there with our camera when the bank started to foreclose on the modest home of the other family because they couldn't meet the mortgage payments after dad lost his good-paying manufacturing job. Like millions of Americans, the Stanleys and the Neumanns were playing by the rules and still getting stiffed. By the end of the decade they were running harder but slipping behind, and the gap between them and prosperous America was widening.

What turns their personal tragedy into a political travesty is that they are patriotic. They love this country. But they no longer believe they matter to the people who run the country. When our film opens, both families are watching the inauguration of Bill Clinton on television in 1992. By the end of the decade they were no longer paying attention to politics. They don't see it connecting to their lives. They don't think their concerns will ever be addressed by the political, corporate, and media elites who make up our dominant class. They are not cynical, because they are deeply religious people with no capacity for cynicism, but they know the system is rigged against them. They know this, and we know this. For years now a small fraction of American households have been garnering an extreme concentration of wealth and income while large corporations and financial institutions have obtained unprecedented levels of economic and political power over daily life. In 1960, the gap in terms of wealth between the top 20% and the bottom 20% was 30-fold. Four decades later it is more than 75-fold.

Growing Inequality

Such concentrations of wealth would be far less of an issue if the rest of society were benefiting proportionately. But that's not the case. As the economist Jeff Madrick reminds us, the pressures of inequality on middle and working class Americans are now quite severe. "The strain on working people and on family life, as spouses have gone to work in dramatic numbers, has become significant. VCRs and television sets are cheap, but higher education, health care, public transportation, drugs, housing and cars have risen faster in price than typical family incomes. And life has grown neither calm nor secure for most Americans, by any means." You can find many sources to support this conclusion. I like the language of a small outfit here in New York called the Commonwealth Foundation/Center for the Renewal of American Democracy. They conclude that working families and the poor "are losing ground under economic pressures that deeply affect household stability, family dynamics, social mobility, political participation, and civic life."

Household economics is not the only area where inequality is growing in America. Equality doesn't mean equal incomes, but a fair and decent society where money is not the sole arbiter of status or comfort. In a fair and just society, the commonwealth will be valued even as individual wealth is encouraged.

Thomas Jefferson's Words

Let me make something clear here. I wasn't born yesterday. I'm old enough to know that the tension between haves and have-nots [is] built into human psychology, it is a constant in human history, and it has been a factor in every society. But I also know America was going to be different. I know that because I read Mr. Jefferson's writings, Mr. Lincoln's speeches and other documents in the growing American creed. I presumptuously disagreed with Thomas Jefferson about human equality being self-evident. Where I lived, neither talent, nor opportunity, nor outcomes were equal. Life is rarely fair and never equal. So what could he possibly have meant by that ringing but ambiguous declaration: "All men are created equal"? Two things, possibly. One, although none of us are good, all of us are sacred (Glenn Tinder), that's the basis for thinking we are by nature kin.

Second, he may have come to see the meaning of those words through the experience of the slave who was his mistress. As is now widely acknowledged, the hands that wrote "all men are created equal" also stroked the breasts and caressed the thighs of a black woman named Sally Hemings. She bore him six children whom he never acknowledged as his own, but who were the only slaves freed by his will when he died—the one request we think Sally Hemings made of her master. Thomas Jefferson could not have been insensitive to the flesh-and-blood woman in his arms. He had to know she was his equal in her desire for life, her longing for liberty, her passion for happiness.

Distribution of Income and Wealth in the United States, 1998

Distribution of:	Household income	Net worth	Net financial assets
All	100.0%	100.0%	100.0%
Top 1%	16.6	38.1	47.3
Next 9%	24.6	32.9	32.4
Bottom 90%	58.8	29.0	20.2

(Wealth defined as net worth—household assets minus debt.)

Lawrence Mishel et al., *State of Working America, 2002/2003*. Ithaca, NY: Cornell University Press, 2003.

In his book on the Declaration, my late friend Mortimer Adler said Jefferson realized that whatever things are really good for any human being are really good for all other human beings. The happy or good life is essentially the same for all: a satisfaction of the same needs inherent in human nature. A just society is grounded in that recognition. So Jefferson kept as a slave a woman whose nature he knew was equal to his. All Sally Hemings got from her long sufferance—perhaps it was all she sought from what may have grown into a secret and unacknowledged love—was that he let her children go. "Let my children go"—one of the oldest of all petitions. It has long been the promise of America—a broken promise, to be sure. But the idea took hold that we could fix what was broken so that our children would live a bountiful life. We could prevent the polarization between the very rich and the very poor that poisoned other societies. We could provide that each and every citizen would enjoy the basic necessities of life, a voice in the system of self-government, and a better chance for their children. We could preclude the vast divides that produced the turmoil and tyranny of the very countries from which so many of our families had fled.

We were going to do these things because we understood our dark side—none of us is good—but we also understood the other side—all of us are sacred. From Jefferson forward we have grappled with these two notions in our collective head— that we are worthy of the creator but that power corrupts and absolute power corrupts absolutely. Believing the one and knowing the other, we created a country where the winners didn't take all. Through a system of checks and balances we were going to maintain a safe, if shifting, equilibrium between wealth and commonwealth. We believed equitable access to public resources is the lifeblood of any democracy. So early on . . . primary schooling was made free to all. States changed laws to protect debtors, often the relatively poor, against their rich creditors. Charters to establish corporations were open to most, if not all, white comers, rather than held for the elite. The government encouraged Americans to own their own piece of land, and even supported squatters' rights. The court challenged monopoly—all in the name of we the people.

In my time we went to public schools. My brother made it to college on the GI bill. When I bought my first car for $450 I drove to a subsidized university on free public highways and stopped to rest in state-maintained public parks. This is what I mean by the commonwealth. Rudely recognized in its formative years, always subject to struggle, constantly vulnerable to reactionary counterattacks, the notion of America as a shared project has been the central engine of our national experience.

A Profound Transformation

Until now. I don't have to tell you that a profound transformation is occurring in America: the balance between wealth and the commonwealth is being upended. By design. Deliberately. We have been subjected to what the Commonwealth Foundation calls "a fanatical drive to dismantle the political institutions, the legal and statutory canons, and the intellectual and cultural frameworks that have shaped public responsibility for social harms arising from the excesses of private power." From land, water and other natural resources, to media and the broadcast and digital spectrums, to scientific discovery and medical breakthroughs, and to politics itself, a broad range of the American commons is undergoing a powerful shift toward private and corporate control. And with little public debate. Indeed, what passes for 'political debate' in this country has become a cynical charade behind which the real business goes on—the not-so-scrupulous business of getting and keeping power in order to divide up the spoils. . . .

Economic Inequality and Political Inequality

So what does this come down to, practically?

Here is one accounting:

> When powerful interests shower Washington with millions in campaign contributions, they often get what they want. But it's ordinary citizens and firms that pay the price and most of them never see it coming. This is what happens if you don't contribute to their campaigns or spend generously on lobbying. You pick up a disproportionate share of America's tax bill. You pay higher prices for a broad range of products from peanuts to prescriptions. You pay taxes that others in a similar situation have been excused from paying. You're compelled to abide by laws while others are granted immunity from them. You must pay debts that you incur while others do not. You're barred from writing off on your tax returns some of the money spent on necessities while others deduct the cost of their entertainment. You must run your business by one set of rules, while the government creates another set for your competitors. In contrast, the fortunate few who contribute to the right politicians and hire the right lobbyists enjoy all the benefits of their special status. Make a bad business deal; the government bails them out. If they want to hire workers at below market wages, the government provides the means to do so. If they want more time to pay their debts, the government gives them an extension. If they want immunity from certain laws, the government gives it. If they want to ignore rules their competition must comply with, the government gives its approval. If they want to kill legislation that is intended for the public, it gets killed.

I'm not quoting from Karl Marx's *Das Kapital* or Mao's *Little Red Book*. I'm quoting *Time* magazine. Time's premier investigative journalists—Donald Bartlett and James Steele—concluded in a series last year (2003) that America now has "government for the few at the expense of the many." Economic inequality begets political inequality, and vice versa.

That's why the Stanleys and the Neumanns were turned off by politics. It's why we're losing the balance between wealth and the commonwealth. It's why we can't put things right. And it is the single most destructive force tearing at the soul of democracy. Hear the great justice Learned Hand on this: "If we are to keep our democracy, there must be one commandment: 'Thou shalt not ration justice.'" Learned Hand was a prophet of democracy. The rich have the right to buy more homes than anyone else. They have the right to buy more cars than anyone else, more gizmos than anyone else, more clothes and vacations than anyone else. But they do not have the right to buy more democracy than anyone else.

Class War

I know, I know: this sounds very much like a call for class war. But the class war was declared a generation ago, in a powerful paperback polemic by William Simon, who was soon to be Secretary of the Treasury. He called on the financial and business class, in effect, to take back the power and privileges they had lost in the depression and New Deal. They got the message, and soon they began a stealthy class war against the rest of society and the principles of our democracy. They set out to trash the social contract, to cut their workforces and wages, to scour the globe in search of cheap labor, and to shred the social safety net that was supposed to protect people from hardships beyond their control.

The middle class and working poor are told that what's happening to them is the consequence of [economist] Adam Smith's "Invisible Hand." This is a lie. What's happening to them is the direct consequence of corporate activism, intellectual propaganda, the rise of a religious orthodoxy that in its hunger for government subsidies has made an idol of power, and a string of political decisions favoring the powerful and the privileged who bought the political system right out from under us. . . .

Let's face the reality: If ripping off the public trust; if distributing tax breaks to the wealthy at the expense of the poor; if driving the country into deficits deliberately to starve social benefits; if requiring states to balance their budgets on the backs of the poor; if squeezing the wages of workers until the labor force resembles a nation of serfs—if this isn't class war, what is?

It's un-American. It's unpatriotic. And it's wrong.

> "*Egalitarianism is . . . an absurd attempt to deny in the name of justice that people should be . . . treated as they deserve based on their merits or demerits.*"

Efforts to Promote Economic Equality Are Misguided

John Kekes

John Kekes, a former philosophy professor at the State University of New York at Albany, is the author of many books, including *The Illusions of Egalitarianism* and *Against Liberalism: A Case for Conservatism*. In the following viewpoint he criticizes the view that justice requires society to take steps to promote economic equality. Such a view of social justice ignores the place of individual responsibility and effort in determining whether people have what they deserve, he contends. He further argues that most Americans already share enough with the truly poor through their taxes and contributions to charities. According to Kekes, taxing the wealthy and redistributing wealth to the poor would weaken America's economic system, which has created much wealth and made poverty a relatively small problem.

As you read, consider the following questions:

1. What absurdities does Kekes argue follow logically from egalitarianism?
2. How does the author respond to the question of whether it is evil that individuals' prospects at birth can differ so radically?
3. What evidence does Kekes present in support of his view that the poor are being treated fairly in American society?

E galitarians believe that inequality is unjust and justice requires a society to move steadily toward greater equality. This is the aim and the justification of proportional taxation, affirmative action, equal opportunity programs, and of the whole panoply of anti-poverty policies that bring us ever closer to the socialist dream of a welfare state. These policies cost money. The egalitarian approach to getting it is to tax those who have more in order to benefit those who have less. The absurdity of this is that egalitarians suppose that justice requires ignoring whether people deserve what they have and whether they are responsible for what they lack. They suppose it just to ignore the requirements of justice.

Consequences of Egalitarianism

Here is a consequence of egalitarianism. According to the *Statistical Abstract of the United States*, men's life expectancy is on the average about 7 years less than women's. There is thus an inequality between men and women. If egalitarians mean it when they say that "it would be a better state of affairs if everyone enjoyed the same level of social and economic benefits," or that "how could it not be an evil that some people's prospects at birth are radically inferior to others," then they must find the inequality between the life expectancy of men and women unjust. As they say, "those who have been favored by nature . . . may gain from their good fortune only in terms that improve the situation of those who have lost out."

Egalitarians, thus, must see it as a requirement of justice to equalize the life expectancy of men and women. This can be done, for instance, by men having more and better health care than women; by employing fewer men and more women in stressful or hazardous jobs; and by men having shorter work days and longer vacations than women. Such policies will not diminish productivity if loss in man-hours is compensated for by gain in woman-hours.

Yet a further policy follows from the realization that since men have shorter lives than women, they are less likely to benefit after retirement from Social Security and Medicare. As things are, in their present inegalitarian state, men and women are required to contribute an equal percentage of their earnings to Social Security and Medicare. This is clearly unjust from the egalitarian point of view: Why should men be required to subsidize the health and wealth of women? The policy this suggests is to decrease the levy on men, or increase it on women, or possibly do both at once. There is thus much that egalitarian policies could do to reduce the unjust inequality in the life expectancy of men and women.

However much that is, it will affect only future generations. There remains the question of how to compensate the present generation of men for the injustice of having shorter lives than women. No compensation can undo the damage, but it may make it easier to bear. The obvious policy is to set up preferential treatment programs designed to provide for men at least some of the benefits they would have enjoyed had their life expectancy been equal to women's. There is a lot of pleasure that could be had in those 7 years that men are not going to have. And since those years would have come at the end of their lives, when they are more likely to know their minds, their loss affects not only the quantity but also the quality of their not-to-be-had pleasures. One efficient way of compensating them for their loss is to set up government sponsored pleasure centers in which men may spend the hours and days gained from having shorter working days and longer vacations.

Can These Absurdities Be Avoided?

These absurd policies follow from egalitarianism, and their absurdity casts doubt on the beliefs from which they follow. This ought to lead to the suspicion that the policies more usually associated with egalitarianism, namely anti-poverty programs, various welfare legislations, proportional taxation, the preferential treatment of minorities and women, and so forth, suffer from analogous absurdity. One may actually come to suspect that the familiar egalitarian policies do not appear absurd only because they are made familiar by endlessly repeated mind-numbing rhetoric that disguise the lack of reasons for them.

Can egalitarians avoid these absurdities? They might claim that there is a significant difference between the unequal life expectancy of men and women, and the inequality of rich and poor, whites and blacks, or men and women in respects other than life expectancy. The difference, egalitarians might say, is that the poor, blacks, and women are unequal as a result of injustice, such as exploitation, discrimination, prejudice, and so forth, while this is not true of the life expectancy of men.

Income Inequality: So What?

There's a deeper point about income inequality, which can be summarized as "so what?" Since when is disparity between incomes the only gauge of how good a state of affairs is? If all philosophy professors could double their incomes, but only as part of some scheme whereby history professors would triple theirs, is it not in my interest to agree to this? There's a sense in which this may be "unfair," but preferring the status quo is clearly detrimental, to me as well as to everyone else. If all the historians start driving Jaguars, I have still doubled my income. It's more a matter of attitude whether I am filled with joy at the increase in my wealth or resentful that the historians have even more. I prefer the former. The latter is psychologically, as well as socially, destructive. If one approach to political economy makes both Smith and Jones richer, but to different degrees, that is preferable to one in which both are equally impoverished. So to lament inequality without taking into consideration real gains by all is morally obtuse at best. At worst, it's deceitful.

Aeon J. Skoble, *Freeman*, October 2002.

A moment of thought shows, however, that this claim is untenable. The group of men includes blacks and the poor who, according to egalitarians, have suffered from injustice in the past. And blacks and women include high achievers, middle and upper class people, people with considerable wealth, as well as recent immigrants who came to this country voluntarily and who could not have suffered from past injustice here. It is but the crudest prejudice to think of men as Archie Bunkers, of women as great talents sentenced to housewifery, and of blacks as ghetto dwellers doomed by injustice to a life of poverty, crime, and addiction. Many men have been victims of injustice, and many women and blacks have not suffered from it.

It will be said against this that there still is a difference because the poor, blacks, and women are more likely to have been victims of injustice than men. Suppose this is true. What justice requires then, according to egalitarians, is to redistribute resources to them and to compensate them for their loss. But these policies will be just only if they benefit victims of injustice, and the victims cannot be identified simply as poor, blacks, or women because they, as individuals, may not have suffered any injustice. Moreover, those members of these groups who do lack resources may do so, not because of injustice, but because of bad luck, personal defects, or having taken risks and lost. Overcoming injustice requires, therefore, a much more precise identification of the victims than merely membership in such amorphous groups as those of women, blacks or the poor. This more precise identification requires asking and answering the question of why specific individuals are in a position of inequality.

People Create Their Own Fate

Answering it, however, must include consideration of the possibility that people may cause or contribute to their own misfortune and that it is their lack of merit, effort, or responsibility, not injustice, that explains their position. Egalitarians, however, ignore this possibility. According to them, the mere fact of inequality is sufficient to warrant redistribution and compensation. They say, for instance, that "a distribution of wealth that dooms some citizens to a less fulfilling life than others, no matter what choices they make, is unacceptable, and the neglect of equality in contemporary politics is therefore shameful." Regardless [of] whether egalitarians are right about this, they face a dilemma. If the policies of redistribution and compensation do take into account the degree to which people are responsible for being in a position of inequality, then the justification of these policies must go beyond what egalitarians can provide. For the justification must involve consideration of the choices people make, as well as their merit, effort, responsibility. To the extent to which this is done, the justification ceases to be egalitarian.

If, on the other hand, the policies of redistribution and compensation do not take into account the responsibility people have for their inequality, then there is no difference between the inequality of men and women in respect to life expectancy, and the poor, blacks, and women who are unequal in other respects. Consistent egalitarian policies would then have to aim to overcome all inequalities, and that is just what produces the absurd policies noted above.

Egalitarians may try to avoid absurdity in another way. They may say, "how could it not be an evil that some people's prospects at birth are radically inferior to others?" The expectation is that the question will be regarded as rhetorical, since the answer to it will be obvious, at least to right-minded people. This expectation, however, is mistaken. That some people's prospects at birth are radically inferior to others is a statistical necessity. Being a necessity, it holds in all societies, even in a socialist heaven. Given any population and any basis of ranking the prospects of individuals in the population, some will rank higher and others lower. Those who rank lowest will have prospects radically inferior to those who rank highest. Complaining about this unavoidable fact of life is as reasonable as lamenting differences in height or weight. To call this statistical necessity evil is a sentimental cheapening of the most serious condemnation language affords. And the refusal to call it evil shows respect for facts rather than insensitivity.

A Nagging Doubt

Suppose that egalitarianism is seen for what it is: an absurd attempt to deny in the name of justice that people should be held responsible for their actions and treated as they deserve based on their merits or demerits. A nagging doubt remains. It is undeniable that there are in our society innocent victims of misfortune and injustice. Their inequality is not their fault, they are not responsible for it, and they do not deserve to be in a position of inequality. The emotional appeal of egalitarianism is that it recognizes the plight of these people and proposes ways of helping them. Counting on the compassion of decent people, egalitarians then charge their society with injustice for ignoring the suffering of innocent victims.

There are several things that need to be said in response to this frequently heard charge. First, anyone committed to justice will want people to have what they deserve and not to have what they do not deserve. Innocent victims do not deserve to suffer, yet they do. A decent society should do what it can to alleviate their suffering. But this has nothing to do with equality or egalitarianism. What is objectionable is not that some people have less than others. It is not unjust that millionaires have less than billionaires. What is objectionable is that some people, through no fault of their own, lack the basic necessities of nutrition, health care, education, housing, and so forth. They are our fellow citizens, and because of that we feel compassion for their plight.

Second, the plight of innocent victims who lack the basic necessities is not ignored. On the contrary, they are being helped by their fellow citizens who are taxpayers. Take a family of four with an annual income of $70,000. They are likely to pay about $25,000 in federal, state, property, and school taxes. Approximately 60 percent of the federal and state budget is spent on social programs. Thus roughly 60 percent of the family's annual taxes, that is, $15,000, is spent on social programs. The family, therefore, contributes over 20 percent of their income, more than one dollar out of every five, to helping others, including the innocent victims. This is more than enough to acquit them of the charge of shamefully ignoring the plight of their fellow citizens that egalitarians baselessly level against them.

Third, the relentless egalitarian propaganda eagerly parroted by the media would have us believe that our society is guilty of dooming people to a life of poverty. What this ignores is the unprecedented success of our society in having less than 13 percent of the population live below a very generously defined poverty level and 87 percent above it. The typical ratio in past societies is closer to the reverse. It is a cause for celebration, not condemnation, that for the first time in history a very large segment of the population has escaped poverty. If egalitarians had a historical perspective, they would be in favor of the political and economic system that has made this possible, rather than advocating absurd policies that undermine it.

"The death tax is unfair, unnecessary, and doesn't work either as a significant revenue raiser . . . or a valuable social policy for American society."

Repealing the Estate Tax Is Just

Citizens for a Sound Economy

Citizens for a Sound Economy (CSE) is an activist organization that advocates limited government; it merged with another organization in 2004 and changed its name to FreedomWorks. In the following viewpoint, taken from a 2000 publication, it claims that the federal estate tax—what it calls the "death tax"—is fundamentally unfair because it penalizes society's achievers by preventing them from bequeathing their assets to their family or other loved ones. Moreover, the organization claims, the tax often results in double or triple taxation of certain individuals, which is unjust. Such taxes destroy the American dream and should be repealed, it argues.

As you read, consider the following questions:
1. Why is "death tax" an appropriate name for the estate tax, according to CSE?
2. Why is the death tax unnecessary, according to the author?
3. What examples does the author give of how the estate tax affects people's lives?

Citizens for a Sound Economy, *A Citizen's Guide to the Death Tax*, www. freedomworks.org, 2000. Copyright © 2000 by the Americans for Prosperity Foundation. Reproduced by permission.

Federal politicians' insatiable desire to tax private citizens is nowhere more clearly demonstrated than in the spectacle of the Internal Revenue Service (IRS) seizing taxes that are owed for no other reason than the fact that an American has died. Whether they are called federal "transfer taxes," "estate taxes" or "death taxes," they amount to the same thing: the government seizing American citizens' property at their death instead of allowing them to pass a legacy on to family or other loved ones as they see fit.

We make no bones about our assertion that the estate or federal transfer tax should rightly be called the "death tax," since the death of an American is the only event that can trigger the government's claim on this property. Neither do we shrink from our claim that the death tax is unfair, unnecessary, and doesn't work either as a significant revenue raiser for the government or a valuable social policy for American society.

The "gift tax" serves as the death tax's partner in crime. The gift tax is designed by the same politicians who brought us the death tax as a way to make sure Americans can't pass along their property to family or loved ones as a "gift" while the gift-givers are alive. The gift tax is just as unfair, just as unnecessary, and just as unworkable as the death tax.

Americans must reclaim their right to have the government as well as their heirs honor their last wishes at death. Americans pay payroll and income taxes all their working lives as well as sales and property taxes on real property. To pay nearly half of what we earn, purchase, or hold, only to have the government claim a right to tax whatever is left a final time at our death should shock all of us into standing up and saying "Enough."

We may be used to seeing the government do things that don't work and that are unnecessary. But the death tax and its partner, the gift tax, go further. They are unfair and wrong. And they should be repealed.

The Death Tax Is Unnecessary

Despite raising just slightly more than 1 percent of all federal revenues, the collection of death taxes is very expensive. According to one study, total compliance costs (including economic disincentives) amount to about 65 cents for every dollar that is collected. For example, in 1997, the death tax raised $20 billion. But the cost of the government collecting those taxes combined with the costs of individuals complying with those tax laws was another $12 billion. This means that the $20 billion the IRS collected required a $32 billion drain on the economy. Conversely, repealing the death tax would cost the government only $20 billion, but would constitute a $32 billion boost to the economy.

The Death Tax Is Unfair

Chester Thigpen is an 86-year-old tree farmer in Mississippi. Mr. Thigpen, a grandson of slaves, and wife, Rosett, have raised five children on their tree farm. Starting in 1990, Mr. Thigpen bought a little land to start his own farm. Through hard work and sacrifice, he has built an 850-acre farm that is worth more than $1 million. Despite this great accomplishment, the Thigpens are far from comparison with the Rockefellers. As Chester's son Lonnie noted in his testimony before Congress: "We're not rich people. My father and I do almost all of the work on our land ourselves. . . . My father and I planted some more trees not long ago. He knows he will not likely be here to see them mature. But he hopes that his grandchildren and great grandchildren will be able to watch these trees grow on the Thigpen Tree Farm." Unfortunately, when Chester Thigpen dies, his heirs will have to pay the U.S. government up to 55 percent of his net worth. Most likely, his children will be forced to sell some of the precious land and some of the trees planted by Mr. Thigpen to meet the death tax bill. It's somewhat ironic that the same government that freed his grandparents from the bonds of slavery will force his own grandchildren to liquidate the family farm. . . .

Death taxes confiscate anywhere from 37 percent to 55 percent of Americans' savings upon their death, once the $650,000 threshold is met. Besides being the steepest tax rates in the tax code, the death tax is blatantly unfair in that it represents double and maybe even triple taxation on the same dollar. For instance, consider the case of Mike Rogers. Every time Mr. Rogers, an owner of a small industrial manufacturing firm, gets paid, federal, state, and local taxes are taken out

Asay. © 2002 by Creators Syndicate, Inc. Reproduced by permission.

of his paycheck. Then he places a small amount of his take-home pay into a stock fund. When he sells a stock at a profit, his same dollar is again taxed at the capital gains tax rate (20 percent). Finally, when he dies and attempts to leave his life savings and business to his son or daughter, he will be subject to a death tax on all assets at a rate that can reach 55 percent. Because most of his business investment is wrapped up in expensive machinery, Mr. Rogers' estate will exceed the $650,000 threshold even though no one would know it by looking at the modest home and dilapidated car he owns. It is simply not fair to tax the same dollar of income two, three, or even four times. One time should be enough for Uncle Sam.

Not Just the Rich

There's an old saying, often repeated by President Ronald Reagan, that "in the end, you don't tax things, you tax people." That is, a "property tax" doesn't tax the house, it taxes the homeowner and his or her family. Likewise, a tariff doesn't tax the imported television set, it taxes the American who purchases it. It is in this sense that the death tax doesn't so much hit the American who has died or the estate they have left so much as it hits those who would receive the estate.

Say, for instance, an American owns 20 hardware stores worth a total of about $500,000 each, making his business worth $10 million. And suppose we call this American "rich." What if that hardware store owner decides that, when he dies, a certain manager who has worked hard and been loyal to the business for 20 years deserves to be given ownership of the store he's managed. Sure, the owner of the hardware stores is rich. But the store manager is not rich at all. If, when the owner dies, his estate is taxed at a 37 percent rate, that would mean the loyal store manager wouldn't get ownership of the store free and clear. Instead, the manager would have to either sell the store to a new owner who could afford the tax, or somehow come up with the 37 percent (or $185,000) in taxes before he could really own the store. In this scenario, it's plain to see that it is the loyal store manager of modest means, not the recently deceased rich owner who bears the brunt of the death tax.

Viewed in this way, the very idea that we can tax "the dead" just doesn't make sense, any more than it makes sense to say that we can tax "estates." In the end, you don't tax things, you tax people. And in the case of the death tax, the IRS is taxing people who would otherwise realize the means to seek their own part in the American dream, through the generous help and wishes of one who has died.

The other class-warfare argument put forth by supporters of the death tax is aimed at the "rich" owners of the estate. Death tax supporters cite the $650,000 exemption as proof that the death tax is only charged against the rich. While $650,000 in the bank would be a welcome addition to any-body's nest egg, that amount of savings held in a bank account yielding a 4 percent rate of return would only generate a re-tirement income of $26,000 a year before taxes. At an effec-tive 25 percent income tax rate, that income would provide about $20,000 a year after taxes. For most people, $20,000 a year in take-home pay doesn't make you rich. . . .

Arguments Against the Death Tax

As University of Southern California Law Professor Edward McCaffery, a self-described "unrequited liberal" stated in testimony before the Senate Finance Committee: "[The death tax] discourages behavior that a liberal, democratic society ought to like—work, savings, bequests—and encourages behavior that such a society ought to suspect—the large-scale consumption, leisure, and intervivos giving of the very rich. It is a tax on work and savings without consumption, on thrift, on long-term savings. There is no reason even a liberal populace need support it. The current gift and estate tax does not work, is in deep tension with liberal egalitarian ideals, and lacks strong popular or political support.". . .

Likewise, death taxes only encourage economic behaviors that many observers (including Federal Reserve Chairman Alan Greenspan) have characterized as "the key domestic economic policy problem" of this country—its low savings rate. By penalizing those who work hard, reinvest in their businesses, and leave their children with the opportunity to live a happier and more prosperous life than they themselves did, death taxes only enhance the low savings rate problem of the United States by encouraging consumption at the hands of savings.

*"The estate tax is part of our country's
historic response to excessive inequality."*

Repealing the Estate Tax Is Unjust

William H. Gates Sr. and Chuck Collins

In 2001 Congress voted to gradually reduce the federal estate tax (or "death tax"). In the following viewpoint William H. Gates Sr. and Chuck Collins argue that repealing the federal tax on inheritances is a bad idea for both economic and moral reasons. Without the tax, they claim, state revenues and the services they support will decline. Moreover, the wealthiest citizens in America have the obligation to pay their fair share of taxes for the common good, they argue. Repealing the inheritance tax worsens economic inequality in the United States, they contend. Gates is cochair of the Bill and Melinda Gates Foundation and the father of Microsoft chairman Bill Gates. Collins is cofounder of United for a Fair Economy, an activist organization. Gates and Collins are coauthors of *Wealth and Our Commonwealth: Why America Should Tax Accumulated Fortunes.*

As you read, consider the following questions:
1. How many estates each year are affected by the estate tax, according to Gates and Collins?
2. What "myths" about wealth do the authors attempt to debunk?
3. What examples of religious teachings do Gates and Collins use to support their argument that society has legitimate claims on the wealthy?

In the last several years, Congress has debated whether to eliminate the federal estate tax—or "death tax"—our nation's only levy on accumulated wealth. The paltry debate over elimination of the tax has not grappled adequately with the negative consequences of repealing the estate tax.

One hundred years ago, during the first Gilded Age, we had a rigorous debate about the dangers of concentrated wealth in a democracy. The debate over the estate tax goes to the heart of the question of "what kind of country do we want to become" and ethical questions about society's claim upon the accumulated fortunes of the wealthy.

The Campaign to Repeal the Estate Tax

Ten years ago, a number of wealthy families—including the heirs to the Mars [candy] and Gallo [wine] fortunes—began bankrolling a campaign for wholesale repeal of the tax. Instead of revealing the true beneficiaries of repeal—households in the top 1 percent of wealth holders—they put forward a media campaign representing farmers and small-business owners as injured parties to the tax. Much of this mythmaking, however, has obscured the dangerous impact of eliminating the tax.

Proponents of repeal argue that the estate tax is un-American, that it punishes success and discourages parents from passing on wealth and businesses to their children. They successfully included elimination of the estate tax in President [George W.] Bush's Tax Relief Act of 2001, through which the estate tax would gradually be phased out and then repealed for one year in 2010. Now repeal advocates are pressing to permanently eliminate the estate tax.

Benefits of the Estate Tax

Why preserve the estate tax? The tax generates substantial revenue to pay for government. These funds are raised from those most able to pay—households in the richest 1 percent. Between now [2003] and 2009, the amount of wealth exempted prior to paying the tax will rise to $3.5 million. Based on recent IRS [Internal Revenue Service] data, that means that only about 6,000 estates a year will pay the tax, with an average estate valued at more than $21 million. Eliminating the revenue from the estate tax will shift the tax burden off those most able to pay onto everyone else or lead to cuts in services for those most in need.

Many states have state-level inheritance or estate taxes that are linked to the federal estate tax. Repeal of the federal estate tax may lead to a severe drop in revenue for states—an estimated $5 billion—at a time when they can ill afford the loss. Almost every state in the country is grappling with severe budget deficits and many are cutting lifeline social programs for low- and middle-income people.

The estate tax serves as a catalyst for charitable giving. Many people give to their religious congregation, community organizations, and other charities regardless of the tax advantages. But evidence suggests the estate tax encourages wealthy households to give even more, particularly households with wealth higher than $20 million. Bequests motivated by the estate tax go toward creation or capitalization of foundations, medical and research organizations, and religious organizations. A U.S. Treasury Department report estimates that charitable giving will drop by $6 billion a year without an estate tax incentive.

The estate tax is part of our country's historic response to excessive inequality. The American experiment is rooted in a suspicion of concentrated wealth and power and in the rejection of aristocracy. The estate tax was established in 1916 as a populist response to the excesses of the Gilded Age. At a time when the gap between the very rich and everyone else is once again at historic levels, it seems un-American to eliminate the one tax that discourages the build-up of dynastic wealth holdings.

Society's Claim on the Wealthy

Society has an enormous claim upon the fortunes of the wealthy. This is rooted not only in most religious traditions, but also in an honest accounting of society's substantial investment in creating the fertile ground for wealth-creation.

One of the dominant myths of our time is the "great man" theory of wealth creation—the notion that one's individual success is rooted entirely in one's own effort. You can hear these sentiments in debates over taxes: "I made this money on my own" and "The government has no right to my money." It is important to affirm and celebrate the role of the individual in the creation of wealth and successful enterprises. One significant reason that some people accumulate great wealth is through their hard work, creativity, tenacity, and sacrifice. Individuals do make a difference.

Yet it is equally important to acknowledge the role of a wide variety of influential factors such as luck, privilege, other people's efforts, and society's investment in the creation of individual wealth. The notion of a "self-made millionaire" or "I made this money without any help" is hubris. It is an example of extreme individualism that runs counter to ethical and religious traditions.

Religious Teachings on Property and Charity

Judaism, Christianity, and Islam all affirm the right of individual ownership and private property, but there are moral limits imposed on absolute private ownership of wealth and property. Each tradition affirms that we are not individuals alone but exist in community—a community that makes claims upon us. The notion that "it is all mine" is a violation of these teachings and traditions.

In the Jewish tradition of *tzedakah*, owners of property are required to care for those in need. This is not a matter of charity or choice—it is an obligation. Individual wealth is provided by God, observes business ethicist Meir Tamari, and it is not meant only for the needs and wants of the private owner but is also meant to be used to satisfy the needs of the poor. Tamari believes society acquires a property right in the wealth of the individual to provide, through compulsory acts of taxation, the social and charitable needs of its members.

The moral basis of welcoming and providing for the stranger is in the Hebrew people's experience of being strangers and slaves in the land of Egypt. This memory acknowledges that the Hebrew people would still be oppressed and in Egypt but for the grace of God. The notion "this is all mine" is inconsistent with Jewish law and may be the sin related to the mark of the "people of Sodom." Tamari observes, "The Sodomite view of absolute private property rejects any obligations to assist others, which is contrary to the

45

Jewish concept of limited private-property rights."

The muslim approach to charity includes *zakat*, a compulsory component, and *sadaqa*, voluntary giving. *Zakat* is rooted in the individual's obligation as a member of a community. The prophet Muhammad wrote, "Like the organs of the body, if one suffers then all others rally in response." Joseph Singer, author of *The Edges of the Field: Lessons on the Obligations of Ownership*, notes that *zakat* "represents the unbreakable bond between members of the community." Since all wealth is owned by God and held by humans in trust, owners of property are not allowed to consider their interests alone.

Historical Reasons for the Estate Tax

The estate tax was meant to do more than bolster budgets and aid charities. From its inception, it was meant to ward off the emergence of a hereditary aristocracy in the United States. Established in 1916, the tax was a populist response to the excesses of the Gilded Age. President Theodore Roosevelt justified it by arguing that society has a claim upon the fortunes of its wealthy. Roosevelt pointed out that "most great civilized countries have an income tax and an inheritance tax. In my judgment both should be part of our system of federal taxation." Such taxation, he noted, should "be aimed merely at the inheritance or transmission in their entirety of those fortunes swollen beyond all healthy limits."

A number of modern-day millionaires—who are themselves subject to the tax—understand its historical importance. . . .

Investor Warren Buffett argued in the *New York Times* that repealing the estate tax would be comparable to "choosing the 2020 Olympic team by picking the eldest sons of the gold-medal winners in the 2000 Olympics. . . . Without the estate tax, you in effect will have an aristocracy of wealth, which means you pass down the ability to command the resources of the nation based on heredity rather than merit."

Rosie Hunter and Chuck Collins, *Dollars & Sense*, January/February 2003.

This notion is similar to the principle of stewardship in the Christian tradition. Riches are granted as a gift from God and humans are expected to be responsible stewards of this wealth, including sharing it with those less fortunate. Author and Harvard professor Peter J. Gomes notes, "Upon those who have wealth, there is a burden of responsibility to use it wisely and not only for themselves." The wealthy must be "generous in proportion to their wealth" because "to whom much is given much is expected."

The Catholic bishops have reiterated the notion that there is a "social mortgage on capital"—another way to express society's claim. They affirm the importance of private property and ownership as opposed to statist or collectivist approaches. Yet they balance fundamental American aspirations of freedom and obligation with society's claim on capital.

Support of private ownership does not mean that anyone has the right to unlimited accumulation of wealth. Private property does not constitute for anyone an absolute or unconditioned right. No one is justified in keeping for her exclusive use what she does not need, when others lack necessities. In the American bishops' pastoral *Economic Justice for All*, they noted, "[Owners and managers] have benefited from the work of many others and from the local communities that support their endeavors." Pope John Paul II, in the encyclical *On Human Work*, wrote that capital "is the result of work and bears the signs of human labor." Those who have labored hold a claim to accumulated wealth and capital.

As Americans we are more inclined to enshrine individual success and undervalue these other components in wealth building. But for the good of the country, we need to better account for the true origins of wealth and success.

America's Social Framework

Consider the many components of the social framework that enables great wealth to be built in the United States: a patent system, enforceable contracts, open courts, property ownership records, protection against crime and external threats, public education, and so on. Even the stock market is a form of society-created wealth, providing liquidity to enterprises. When faith in the system is shaken it is clear what happens to individual wealth. . . .

This is a matter that goes beyond the discussion of the estate tax. We must recognize that society has a legitimate claim upon the wealth of the wealthy. It is not simply a matter of charitable giving to institutions that have made a difference to us, such as schools and libraries. It is also an obligation to pay taxes, to pay for the public institutions that foster equality of opportunity, and to give others the opportunities that we've had. It goes to the heart of how we think about ourselves, as individuals and as a society.

Society's claim on individual accumulated wealth is a fundamentally American notion, rooted in recognition of society's direct and indirect investment in an individual's success. In other words, we didn't get here on our own.

*"A constitutional amendment to guarantee
every person the right to a job at a living
wage addresses . . . the economic injustice
of tens of millions of poor people in the
richest country in world history."*

The United States Should Enact a Living Wage Law to Help the Poor

Bill Quigley

In the viewpoint that follows, Bill Quigley, a law professor at Loyola University School of Law in New Orleans, calls for amending the Constitution to mandate a living wage for all workers. He contends that millions of people in the United States work hard yet still do not make enough to escape poverty. Most Americans agree that people who want to work full-time should have the opportunity to obtain jobs that pay enough to support themselves and their families. A living wage amendment would be a step toward economic justice in the United States, he concludes. Quigley is author of the book *Ending Poverty as We Know It: Guaranteeing a Right to a Job at a Living Wage*.

As you read, consider the following questions:
1. What has been the historical response of American society to poverty, according to Quigley?
2. How does Quigley respond to the argument that a living wage law would be too costly and would wreck the free market?

Bill Quigley, "Ending Poverty by Creating a Constitutional Amendment," *Jurist*, September 24, 2002. Copyright © 2002 by William P. Quigley. Reproduced by permission.

> "Our nation, so richly endowed with natural resources and with a capable and industrious population, should be able to devise ways and means of insuring to all our able-bodied working men and women, a fair day's pay for a fair day's work."
>
> —Franklin Delano Roosevelt. May 24, 1937

David Duke[1] was invited by my students to talk to my Law and Poverty class in the early 1990s about welfare, work and poverty. He spoke smoothly about welfare and the laziness of poor people. He easily fielded all student questions. Except one.

The answer to poverty, Duke said repeatedly, was for people to get a job.

"But in Louisiana," said one student, "there are like two hundred thousand children on welfare—but there are several hundred thousand more children who receive free or reduced school lunches. That means that their parents are working and they are still poor. If you say the answer to poverty is work, what do you say to the hundreds of thousands of people in Louisiana who are already working but are still poor?"

For once, David Duke was silent. He had no answer. Finally, he recovered and launched into an attack on cheaters in the school lunch program.

Unfortunately, our country is in much the same situation as David Duke.

A Proposed Amendment

Historically, our first response to poverty has been to advise the poor to work. But if the poor are already working or cannot find a job, what is the next response? Usually, our response is also silence. . . .

A constitutional amendment to guarantee every person the right to a job at a living wage addresses our silence about the economic injustice of tens of millions of poor people in the richest country in world history. With this amendment, every single person who wants to work gets a job. And every

---

1. David Duke, a former member of the Ku Klux Klan, was elected to the state legislature of Louisiana in 1989; the controversial politician later unsuccessfully ran for governor.

worker earns a living wage—at least double the current minimum wage, higher for people with kids.

Around thirty million people in our country work and earn less than $8.50 an hour. Another ten to fifteen million people are looking for work or are working part-time and would like to be working full-time. These people cannot pay all their bills all the time. That is real poverty.

Two Questions

I continually raise two questions about work and poverty when I speak to groups. "Do you believe that people who want to work should have the opportunity to do so?" and "Do you think that people who work full-time should earn enough to be able to support themselves and their families?" Everyone answers yes. Despite different politics, different races, different ages and income levels, people agree that every person should have the chance to work if they want to, and those who work should earn enough to support themselves and their families.

But somewhere along the way we have lowered our expectations for economic justice in our nation. As a result there is a huge gap between what we believe should happen and what is happening.

Our constitution contains our national promises to each other. We promise to protect free speech. We promise to protect the right to vote. While we have not been able to fulfill these promises perfectly, over time we continue to make progress. As constitutional rights these promises stay on our agenda and we keep working on them. I think the American people are ready to talk about adding a constitutional right to a job at a living wage as a national promise to each other.

Support for a Living Wage

There is already a surprising amount of popular, historical, economic, political, and religious support for a right to a job and for a right to a living wage. There are dozens of energetic and successful local living wage campaigns. Polls show very high support for public job creation and living wages. Many thoughtful economists already support the idea of full employment and living wages. Churches are joining in the calls for living wages and real job opportunity for all.

Critics say that living wages and guaranteeing job opportunities would wreck the "free market." But as any tax lawyer knows, most of those same people are furiously lobbying Congress and state legislatures to change laws to their advantage. The economic system was created by people, is maintained by people, and is constantly being modified by people. Modifying the laws to create job opportunities and living wages is no different a social policy than the $100 billion dollar a year home mortgage deduction which helps people purchase homes and supports the real estate, construction, and banking industries.

Helping the Poor

Why should we help "the poor"? One can say that helping the less fortunate is the moral thing to do, but ideals of Christian charity have a tendency to turn paternalistic. Or, one can make the case that "the poor" put a costly and unnecessary strain on the nation's social fabric that negatively impacts everyone's quality of life. While this is true, viewing poverty as a societal plague takes in only part of the picture. The argument that best holds water acknowledges that the majority of "the poor" are poor not because they don't work, but because society has failed to create an economy that employs all people at a living wage. Consequently, we as a society are collectively responsible for people living in poverty.

Joel Bleifuss, *In These Times*, November 28, 1999.

Cost is also an issue. But a fair discussion about cost has to start with the cost that the American people are now paying to subsidize people working at low-wage jobs and the unemployed. Through our government, our churches, and our families, we now provide assistance for food, healthcare, shelter, and childcare for people who could be self-supporting if given the opportunity. Most people think it is not in our common good that millions are either not working or working and not earning enough to live on. Economic justice for those who are not making ends meet cannot come unless those who are doing well are willing to share to help advance the common good.

It is difficult to amend the constitution and rightfully so.

Our constitution has never before addressed issues of economic justice and the prospect worries some people. But I think a serious national discussion about amending our constitution to provide universal opportunity for jobs and living wages will advance our common good and can lay the groundwork for a permanent national commitment to basic economic justice for all.

Only then can we respond to the silence when confronted with the poverty of millions of our sisters and brothers and only then can we meet the challenge of FDR's call for a fair day's work at a fair day's wage.

*"While trying to solve a non-problem . . .
the living wage crusade creates a very real
problem of low-skilled workers having
trouble finding a job at all."*

A Living Wage Law Would Not Help the Poor

Thomas Sowell

Many cities, in response to church and community activists, have debated ordinances mandating that all workers receive a "living wage." In the following viewpoint, economist and writer Thomas Sowell argues that while a living wage law seems fair in theory, in practice such a law would result in many workers not being able to find jobs at all. Furthermore, he argues that the premise behind the living wage movement—that most people receiving the minimum wage are impoverished heads of families—is not true. Sowell is a senior fellow at the Hoover Institution in Stanford, California. His books include *The Economics and Politics of Race*.

As you read, consider the following questions:
1. What is the political left good at, according to Sowell?
2. What are the consequences of minimum wage laws, according to the author?
3. What subgroups of workers are disproportionately affected by minimum wage laws, according to Sowell?

G ive credit where credit is due. The political left is great with words. Conservatives have never been able to come up with such seductive phrases as the left mass produces.

While conservatives may talk about a need for "judicial restraint," liberals cry out for "social justice." If someone asks you why they should be in favor of judicial restraint, you have got to sit them down and go into a long explanation about constitutional government and its implications and prerequisites.

But "social justice"? No explanation needed. No definition. No facts. Everybody is for it. Do you want social injustice?

A Verbal Coup

The latest verbal coup of the left is the phrase "a living wage." Who is so hard-hearted or mean-spirited that they do not want people to be able to make enough money to live on?

Unfortunately, the effort and talent that the left puts into coining great phrases is seldom put into facts or analysis. The living wage campaign shows that as well.

Just what is a living wage? It usually means enough income to support a family of four on one paycheck. This idea has swept through various communities, churches and academic institutions.

Facts have never yet caught up with this idea and analysis is lagging even farther behind.

First of all, do most low-wage workers actually have a family of four to support on one paycheck? According to a recent (2003) study by the Cato Institute,[1] fewer than one out of five minimum wage workers has a family to support. These are usually young people just starting out.

So the premise is false from the beginning. But it is still a great phrase, and that is apparently what matters, considering all the politicians, academics and church groups who are stampeding all and sundry toward the living wage concept.

Minimum Wage Laws

What the so-called living wage really amounts to is simply a local minimum wage policy requiring much higher pay rates

---

1. Carl F. Horowitz, "Keeping the Poor Poor: The Dark Side of the Living Wage," *Cato Policy Analysis*, no. 493, October 21, 2003.

than the federal minimum wage law. It's a new minimum wage.

Since there have been minimum wage laws for generations, not only in the United States, but in other countries around the world, you might think that we would want to look at what actually happens when such laws are enacted, as distinguished from what was hoped would happen.

The Living Wage Movement Is Harmful

People who push for a living wage insist that the lowest-paid workers are victims of social injustice rectifiable through aggressive political action. They are wrong. The lowest-paid members of the workforce suffer from a lack of skills. In 1994 the Labor and Commerce Departments issued a joint report warning of a widening underclass of workers unable to compete in a complex marketplace. The report spoke of "a large, growing population for whom illegal activity is more attractive than legitimate work.". . .

The living wage campaign is a triumph of confrontation politics and class resentment. By framing the issue as the poor vs. employers, proponents have convinced many local public officials that their campaign is an overdue and unstoppable juggernaut for social justice. It is time for local elected officials to resist a living wage movement that is likely to harm America's poor in the name of protecting them.

Carl F. Horowitz, "Keeping the Poor Poor: The Dark Side of the Living Wage," *Cato Policy Analysis*, no. 493, October 21, 2003.

Neither the advocates of this new minimum wage policy nor the media—much less politicians—show any interest whatsoever in facts about the consequences of minimum wage laws.

Most studies of minimum wage laws in countries around the world show that fewer people are employed at artificially higher wage rates. Moreover, unemployment falls disproportionately on lower skilled workers, younger and inexperienced workers, and workers from minority groups.

The new Cato Institute study cites data showing job losses in places where living wage laws have been imposed. This should not be the least bit surprising. Making anything more expensive almost invariably leads to fewer purchases. That includes labor.

While trying to solve a non-problem—supporting families that don't exist, in most cases—the living wage crusade creates a very real problem of low-skilled workers having trouble finding a job at all.

People in minimum wage jobs do not stay at the minimum wage permanently. Their pay increases as they accumulate experience and develop skills. It increases an average of 30 percent in just their first year of employment, according to the Cato Institute study. Other studies show that low-income people become average-income people in a few years and high-income people later in life.

Killing Jobs

All of this depends on their having a job in the first place, however. But the living wage kills jobs.

As imposed wage rates rise, so do job qualifications, so that less skilled or less experienced workers become "unemployable." Think about it. Every one of us would be "unemployable" if our pay rates were raised high enough.

I would love to believe that the Hoover Institution would continue to hire me if I demanded double my current salary. But you notice that I don't make any such demand. Third parties need to stop making such demands for other people. It is more important for people to have jobs than for busybodies to feel noble.

Periodical Bibliography

The following articles have been selected to supplement the diverse views presented in this chapter.

C.W. Baird	"The Living Wage Folly," *Freeman*, June 2002.
Leon Botstein	"America's Stake in the Estate Tax," *New York Times*, July 23, 2000.
Christian Century	"Is It Fair? Estate Taxes and Wealth Disparities in the United States," December 4, 2002.
Chuck Collins	"Tax Wealth to Broaden Wealth: A Proposal to Tax the Inherited Fortunes of the Rich in Order to Fund a Policy Agenda for Greater Wealth Equality," *Dollars & Sense*, January/February 2004.
Clive Crook	"John Rawls and the Politics of Social Justice," *National Journal*, December 7, 2002.
Economist	"America's Widening Rich-Poor Gap," September 4, 2003.
Bill Gates Sr. and Chuck Collins	"Long Live the Estate Tax!" *Nation*, January 27, 2003.
Kevin A. Hassett	"Rich Man, Poor Man: How to Think About Income Inequality—Hint: It's Not as Bad as You May Think," *National Review*, June 16, 2003.
David Hilfiker	"On Poverty: Despite Massive Wealth, the United States Is Abandoning Its Poor Citizens," *Other Side*, March/April 2004.
Rosie Hunter and Chuck Collins	"Death Tax Deception," *Dollars & Sense*, January/February 2003.
Daniel Kadlec	"Why These Guys Are Dead Wrong: Keep the Estate Tax, Say the Billionaires. Sure—They Can Afford It," *Time*, February 26, 2001.
Paul Krugman	"The Death of Horatio Alger," *Nation*, January 5, 2004.
David Leonhardt	"Time to Slay the Inequality Myth?" *New York Times*, January 25, 2004.
Steven Malanga	"How the 'Living Wage' Sneaks Socialism into Cities," *City Journal*, Winter 2003.
Multinational Monitor	"Inequality and Corporate Power," May 2003.

Jonathan Rowe   "Every Baby a Trust Fund Baby," *American Prospect*, January 1–15, 2001.

Isabel V. Sawhill   "Still the Land of Opportunity?" *Public Interest*, Spring 1999.

Edward Wolff   "The Wealth Divide," *Multinational Monitor*, May 2003.

What Policies Would Promote Social Justice for African Americans?

Chapter Preface

Of the roughly 2 million prisoners held in the United States of America, more than one half, or 1 million, are African American, even though blacks make up less than 13 percent of the U.S. population. A 2003 Department of Justice report found that almost one out of eight black men—12.5 percent—between the ages of twenty and thirty-four were in jail or prison; by comparison, only 1.6 percent of white men in the same age group were incarcerated. The Bureau of Justice Statistics has calculated that 28 percent of black men will be sent to prison or jail in their lifetime. In many states the number of black men in prisons exceeds the number in state universities. Although hundreds of thousands of prisoners are released every year, ex-felons find themselves barred from many jobs and ineligible to vote.

What do these statistics mean? Some observers have seized on the large black population of prisoners and ex-felons as evidence of fundamental social injustice in American society. They note that many African Americans grow up in poor neighborhoods with failing schools, which closes off opportunities other than crime. Others argue that the police concentrate their efforts in urban black communities and that the "war on drugs" seems to be targeting African Americans. To support their contentions these commentators cite studies that have found that while two-thirds of crack cocaine users are white or Hispanic, 84.5 percent of defendants convicted of crack possession in federal court in 1994 were African American. The cumulative result of the high incarceration rate for African Americans has been devastating, these analysts maintain. "For Americans who still believe in racial equality and social justice, we cannot stand silent while millions of our fellow citizens are being destroyed all around us," writes African American studies professor Manning Marable. "The racialized prison industrial complex is the great moral and political challenge of our time."

Others argue that the high incarceration rates of African Americans are not indicative of a racist society but simply reflect existing crime rates. Lawyer Scott W. Johnson argues that sociologists have studied racial disparities in the criminal justice system and have found no evidence of intentional racial discrimination. "It is now widely accepted among serious scholars . . . that higher levels of arrests and incarceration in the U.S. by ethnicity result from higher levels of crime, not racial bias. . . . The black murder rate is seven to ten times the white murder rate." Writes social critic David Horowitz, "The obvious problem [is that] too many blacks are committing crimes."

Whether African Americans are beset by unjust social conditions, or whether crime and other pathologies is the fault of individuals and their choices is a question central to the debates about social justice. The authors in this chapter examine several controversial issues affecting African Americans, including affirmative action programs and slavery reparations, and in doing so present their own views on whether the welfare of African Americans is primarily a social or individual responsibility.

"The . . . persistent structural inequalities that continue to . . . imprison African-American experience are largely outside the parameters of polite public discussion."

African Americans Are Oppressed in American Society

Paul Street

Paul Street is a vice president at the Chicago Urban League; his writings have appeared in *Dissent, Monthly Review,* and other liberal and leftist publications. In the following viewpoint he notes that there is a widespread belief among Americans that racism is a thing of the past and that African Americans no longer face racial barriers. Street disagrees, however, arguing that while explicit and open racial bigotry may no longer be acceptable, black Americans are still victimized by a society that places them in the poorest neighborhoods and schools, leaves them with poorer medical care and economic opportunities, and singles them out for criminal prosecution and incarceration. Those who seek greater social justice in the United States must still confront America's continuing racial divide, he concludes.

As you read, consider the following questions:

1. What is the missing element in the newspaper stories described by Street to begin the viewpoint?
2. According to the author, what are African Americans being conditioned to think about their place in American society?
3. What are the responsibilities of liberals and leftists regarding race, according to Street?

S ometimes it's the silences that speak the loudest. Consider, for example, a study released last year [2001] by a team of public health researchers at the Children's Memorial Hospital in Chicago. As noted in a front-page *Chicago Sun Times* story titled "Danger Zones for Kids," this study reported that injury was the leading cause of death for youth in the United States. The problem is especially great, its authors learned, in Chicago, where injuries killed 106 adolescents per year during the mid-1990s. Especially disturbing was the study's discovery that the city's youth mortality rate for "intentional injury," that is violence, was much higher than for accidental injury. The leading cause of "intentional injury" for Chicago kids over 10 years old was gun violence. Beyond citywide numbers, the researchers reported on the distribution of youth injuries and deaths across the city's 77 officially designated Community Areas. Neighborhood disparities, they found, were severe, ranging from one West Side community where 146 per 100,000 were hospitalized for injuries per year—more than 4 times the citywide average—to more than 30 neighborhoods where fewer than 6 youth were hospitalized for injuries.

Take a front-page *New York Times* piece that appeared late last summer [2001] under the provocative title "Rural Towns Turn to Prisons to Re-ignite Their Economies." According to this article, rural America relies like never before on prison construction to produce jobs and economic development formerly provided by farms, factories, coal mines, and oil. Reporting that 25 new prisons went up in the United States countryside each year during the 1990s, up from 16 per year in the 1980s and just 4 per year in the 1970s, the article quoted an Oklahoma city manager to chilling effect. "There's no more recession-proof form of economic development," this official, whose town just got a shiny new maximum-security prison, told the *Times*, than incarceration because "nothing's going to stop crime."

A final example is provided by another front-page story in the *Chicago Tribune*. Last July [2001], the *Tribune* reported that Ford Heights, a desperately poor "inner-ring" suburb south of Chicago, led the nation in percentage of households headed by single mothers. This article included a map showing the United States' top 20 communities as ranked by percentage of single-mother households. While it related "Ford Heights' dubious title" to residents' poor education, weak job skills, and south-suburban de-industrialization, it especially emphasized residents' "self-defeating social patterns" including, naturally enough, teen sex. Echoing the findings of the latest academic poverty research, it noted a strong connection between teen pregnancy and young people's "hopeless" sense that the future holds little and there is little reason to "defer gratification."

Something Missing

Good, well written reports and articles all. There was something curiously missing, however, from each. Strange though it may seem in one of the world's most racially segregated cities, the Children's Memorial team and the *Sun Times* did not link their findings to readily available, recently released census data on the racial composition of Chicago's neighborhoods. They had to go out of their way not to make the connection. Of the city's top 20 Community Areas ranked by injury-related youth mortality, no less than 15 are currently 90 percent or more African-American. All but one very disproportionately Black for the city. By contrast, more than three-fourths of the 31 neighborhoods where just 6 or less injury-related youth hospitalizations occurred per year were very disproportionately white.

In a similar vein, the *Tribune* piece, while curiously including three photographs of African-American Ford Heights teen moms, refrained from mentioning that all of the top 20 single-mom communities were very disproportionately African-American. Seventy percent of those communities where youth feel especially hopeless are more than 90 percent black. All but one are at least two-thirds black. Nowhere, finally, could the liberal *Times* bring itself to mention the very predominantly white composition of the keepers and the very predominantly black composition of those kept in America's burgeoning new prison towns.

One has to go elsewhere than the nation's leading newspaper to learn that blacks are 12.3 percent of the U.S. population but comprise fully half of the roughly 2 million Americans currently behind bars. . . .

Color Blind

Under the rule of color-blind rhetoric, significant and wide-spread racism is largely a thing of the nation's past. There is a widespread belief among U.S. Whites that African-Americans now enjoy equal opportunity. "As white America sees it," write Leonard Steinhorn and Barbara Diggs-Brown in their sobering *By the Color of Their Skin: The Illusion of Integration and the Reality of Race (2000)*, "every effort has been made to welcome blacks into the American mainstream, and now they're on their own . . . 'We got the message, we made the corrections—get on with it.'"

White Privilege

Few whites have ever thought of our position as resulting from racial preferences. Indeed, we pride ourselves on our hard work and ambition, as if somehow we invented the concepts.

As if we have worked harder than the folks who were forced to pick cotton and build levies for free; harder than the Latino immigrants who spend 10 hours a day in fields picking strawberries or tomatoes; harder than the (mostly) women of color who clean hotel rooms or change bedpans in hospitals, or the (mostly) men of color who collect our garbage.

We strike the pose of self-sufficiency while ignoring the advantages we have been afforded in every realm of activity: housing, education, employment, criminal justice, politics, banking and business. We ignore the fact that at almost every turn, our hard work has been met with access to an opportunity structure denied to millions of others. Privilege, to us, is like water to the fish: invisible precisely because we cannot imagine life without it.

Tim Wise, *Alternet*, February 20, 2003.

In our current officially color-blind era of American history, older and more blatant forms and incidents of classic explicit and intentional racial bigotry are still fit subjects for open discussion. It helps if those forms and incidents are understood as anomalous and identified primarily with lower- and working-class whites who do not understand the new rules of the game. The more significant and persistent structural inequalities that continue to shape, limit, and imprison

African-American experience are largely outside the parameters of polite public discussion. The new reluctance to speak freely about race comes in conservative, liberal, and left forms. For conservatives, predictably, the conventional argument that racism is essentially over and that the main barrier to black advancement comes from within the black community, in the form of self-destructive behaviors and beliefs. There's nothing surprising in this reactionary racist sentiment, which parallels triumphant capitalist "end of history" wisdom on the related and supposed irrelevance of class and other barriers to freedom and democracy in the U.S.

There are now liberals who share the sense that racism has ceased to be a significant barrier to black well being and success. Among liberals, and some further to the left, however, color-blind rhetoric appears more commonly in the argument that society will best serve blacks by downplaying the danger zone of race and emphasizing the shared dilemmas faced by all economically disadvantaged people regardless of color. . . .

Blame the Victim

Whatever form it takes, however, color-blind rhetoric and the "illusion of integration" it conveys render much of America's harshly divided social landscape shockingly unintelligible. The phenomena that are hopelessly muddled include an inequitably funded educational system that apparently just happens to provide poorer instruction for blacks than whites; an electoral system whose voting irregularities and domination by big money happens to disproportionately disenfranchise blacks; a criminal justice system that happens to especially stop, arrest, prosecute, and incarcerate African-Americans; a political economy whose tendency toward sharp inequality happens to especially impoverish and divide black communities; and residential markets and housing practices that happen to disproportionately restrict African-American children to the poorest and most dangerous neighborhoods and communities, where kids' chances of learning are significantly diminished by the threats of injury and violence. The list goes on.

Worse, Americans trained to believe that all the relevant

racial barriers have been torn down are conditioned to think that the nation's millions of truly disadvantaged African-Americans have no one but themselves to blame for their persistent pain and disproportionate presence at the bottom of the American hierarchy. That thought lies at the heart of America's new color-blind racism, which draws ironic strength from the relative decline of acceptable explicit racial bigotry in American life. It is at the core of the hesitancy some liberals and progressives feel about speaking openly on race. It makes well-intentioned anti-racist liberals and leftists reluctant to fully examine the color of modern social problems, for to do so in the current ideological context is, they reason, with some justice, to fuel the fires of new racist (color-blind) victim-blaming and even to damage black self-esteem. . . .

But liberals and leftists will not create the color-blind society of which Martin Luther King so famously dreamed by acting as if it has already arrived. Intellectuals and activists will not answer mainstream denial of racism's deep and stubborn persistence nor respond effectively to the attack on structural understandings of racial inequality by relegating race to the forgotten footnotes. They will carry the moral and political responsibility to write and speak about race and racism as long as skin color continues to significantly shape dominant social, political, and economic structures of opportunity and outcome. To discuss racial differences without reference to cross-racial questions of economic inequality and political economy is to further the racial divide in a way that thwarts social justice and democracy in general.

I "Nobody *is oppressed in America.*"

African Americans Are Not Oppressed in American Society

David Horowitz

Author and civil rights activist David Horowitz is the president of the Center for the Study of Popular Culture. His books include *Hating Whitey and Other Progressive Causes* and *The Politics of Bad Faith.* In the following viewpoint he argues that American society does not oppress African Americans or other minority groups. Rather, he contends, political leftists have a stake in pretending that such racial oppression exists. The pathologies found within black communities, such as high crime and incarceration rates and poor education, cannot be blamed on institutional racism, he argues.

As you read, consider the following questions:
1. Why are people afraid to speak out about the problems of African Americans, according to Horowitz?
2. What is the difference between oppression and bigotry, according to the author?
3. What does the story of Oprah Winfrey say about American society, according to Horowitz?

My book [*Hating Whitey and Other Progressive Causes*] is about race and the double standard that exists in American life. We live in a country where part of the social contract is that it is wrong and unacceptable to be intolerant or to hate another ethnic group. Yet there is a license to hate white people in our culture, and, in fact, the hatred of whites is positively incited at our elite universities.

I got into trouble with these ideas when I wrote a piece for the Internet magazine *Salon*. As a result of that article, Jack White said that I was a racist in his column in *Time* magazine. *Time* actually ran the headline "A Real Live Bigot." It is not pleasant to be called a racist by *Time* magazine, but that is why there is silence on this issue. People are afraid to speak out because they don't want to be called racists. My book is an attempt to speak out, an attempt to provoke a new level of dialog.

A Crippling Message

We have come to a point where if there are too many blacks in jail, the obvious problem—that too many blacks are committing crimes—is not even addressed. It's white racism that accounts for the excessive numbers of blacks in jail. If black kids are not passing tests and are not up to grade level, instead of looking to their parents and their community for a lack of support, or to the schools that are crumbling, we hear that the cause is institutional racism. "Blame whitey" is the idea. Every pathology in the inner-city black communities is blamed on white people.

So, the first thing you can see about this is the crippling message that is being sent to the black community. You have no power to affect your own destiny since white people control everything.

The Left has a vested interest in there being oppressors and oppressed people, and one of the things that really upset Jack White was my statement—which I frequently make when I'm on campuses—that *nobody* is oppressed in America, except maybe children by their abusive parents.

Oppression is a group phenomenon, and there's no way out if you're oppressed. It's different from bigotry, which is an individual matter.

There are millions of refugees from oppressive regimes; that's why we can call them oppressive. They leave their country if they have the freedom to leave. But there's nobody leaving America. There's no exodus from America by black people or brown people. Quite the contrary. They all want to come here. If America is a racist, oppressive country, how come the Haitians want to come here? Why do they want to risk their lives to get to America? To be oppressed? No, once you get the ideological blinders off, and you just think about it for two seconds, you know why they come: They have more rights and more opportunities in America as black Haitians than they do in black-run Haiti. . . .

Public Opinion on White Responsibilities

Question: Do you think the problems that most black Americans face are caused primarily by whites, or don't you think this is the case?

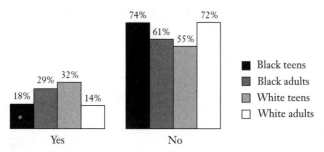

White responsibilities—blacks and whites compared; survey by Yankelovich Partners, Inc., for *Time*/CNN, September 23–October 2, 1997.

Abigail Thernstrom and Stephen Thernstrom, eds., *Beyond the Color Line*, 2002.

I was speaking at Bates College and a young woman asked me, "What about the hierarchies?" Perhaps you're not aware that your children are being taught in every university in America that there are hierarchies of race, class, and gender that oppress designated oppressed groups? So, I said to this young woman, where do you put Oprah Winfrey in your hierarchies? She was the daughter of a Mississippi sharecropper, and she was abused as a child. There was no affirmative action committee telling the television industry that we needed, for diversity purposes, a black female to do a talk show. She clawed her way up, and by her intelligence and her ability, she basically drove Phil Donahue out of the business.

So you can just compact the zillion words of text of all the women's studies courses in America and all of the African-American studies and put them to some better use, because the entire edifice of leftist theory on race and gender is completely demolished by the example of Oprah Winfrey. It's very hard to make a leftist see it, but that is the reality.

"Affirmative action was . . . [a] way of trying to redress the wrongs of the past and prepare the nation for a future of equality."

Affirmative Action Programs Promote Justice for African Americans

E.A. Rohrbach Perry

E.A. Rohrbach Perry is a United Methodist minister in Pennsylvania. In the following viewpoint she argues that affirmative action programs for African Americans are necessary, both to redress past wrongs against African Americans and to counter ongoing discrimination against them. Because many African Americans are still being denied jobs and economic opportunity because of their race, she contends, such programs remain a necessary step toward creating a truly just and equal society.

As you read, consider the following questions:
1. What families does Perry use as examples of continuing racial discrimination in the United States?
2. What percentage of the American public supports affirmative action, according to the author?
3. Why will affirmative action continue to be a hotly debated topic for some time to come, according to Perry?

M arge is 38 and has four children, the oldest is in the Air Force. Over the years, she's had a variety of jobs, everything from baby sitting to janitorial work. The job she liked best was that of a housekeeper at an upscale hotel in her hometown. Permanently laid off after Sept. 11, 2001, she misses that job. "I liked the work. It's easy; I was comfortable with it. I have four kids; I'm used to housekeeping!"

Interviewed in the food pantry waiting room, Marge explained how hard she worked to get that job. She filled out seven applications but was never contacted. Finally, a friend employed by the hotel called her, saying, "Someone didn't show up for work today—I told them you were a hard worker! Get in here fast!" Marge caught a bus to the hotel, filled out her eighth application, and began work that very day.

She thinks it's typical of the area she lives in—if you are a person of color you have to know someone to get a job.

Racial Discrimination

Shirley believes the same thing. She and her husband are an interracial couple and her husband has been having trouble finding work. When they lived in a shoreline resort community, the situation was different she said. The community had an international feel with great diversity of people and her African-American husband was busily employed remodeling homes.

They moved to the northeast because of her mother's declining health and he hasn't been able to find steady employment since then. During good weather, he's been able to get some landscaping work but, during the winter, she brags, "He's a good househusband!"

It's the stereotypes that are holding them back, Shirley thinks. What kind of a place is it where a hard working person can't get a job because the employer makes decisions based on racial stereotypes?

Fifty-four percent of Americans, according to a CBS News/*New York Times* poll, agree that America shouldn't be that kind of place. They support affirmative action programs in employment and educational settings—up 13% from just five years ago [1998]. Only 37% percent of Americans oppose affirmative action—and that number is down 10% from 1998.

Affirmative Action and Justice

America has had over 200 years to deliver true justice, freedom, and equality to women and people of color. To believe that it now will make good the promise of equality without some kind of legislation to assist it is to engage in fantasy.

In advocating for affirmative action policies, people of color are not looking for government handouts. They merely are asking that some mechanism be kept in place to help provide the same social and economic opportunities most whites have had and continue to have access to.

Wilbert Jenkins, *USA Today*, September 1999.

Unfortunately, in that 37% reside some very influential people—the president of the United States, for example. George W. Bush, on Jan. 16 [2003], announced that his administration would support the Supreme Court challenge to the University of Michigan's affirmative action admissions policy. The university uses a point system for admissions and being African American earns applicants a specific number of points. Three Euro-American applicants have filed the case against the university, saying they were denied admissions because the system gives preferences based on race. The president agrees, claiming that the university's system is unconstitutional.[1]

Affirmative Action

The heart of affirmative action lies in the 1965 actions of another president, Lyndon B. Johnson. He introduced the program as a way of addressing discrimination that lingered long after civil rights laws were passed. Of a four-century history in the United States, African Americans spent almost 250 years in slavery and another hundred years in legalized discrimination. Affirmative action was Johnson's way of trying to redress the wrongs of the past and prepare the nation for a future of equality where the American Dream would be available to everyone.

---

1. In June 2003 the Supreme Court ruled that the point system used by the University of Michigan for undergraduate admissions was unconstitutional. But it also upheld a University of Michigan Law School admissions policy that favored minorities, affirming that race can be used in university admission decisions.

In the four decades since Johnson's time, affirmative action has increased opportunities for many people to realize that dream through education and employment. While legalized discrimination died decades ago, racism still lives on. We can see it in the growth of Klan groups, Neo-Nazi groups and hate crimes. (See www.splcenter.org/intelligenceproject/ip-index.html) The affirmative action programs have stood as a continuing attempt to defeat discrimination among those who have not yet understood that racism is not a part of The American Dream.

In that time, affirmative action has also raised criticism that opportunities given to African Americans were being taken away from Euro Americans. Emotive terms like "reverse discrimination," "quotas," and "preferences" were aimed at affirmative action, and the program was accused of giving preferential treatment to people with lower qualifications simply because of their race. Attempts have been made to dismantle the program and the University of Michigan case will most likely be an arena for heightened reactionary rhetoric.

However, the 54% majority of Americans won't be silent, either. "Angry White Guys for Affirmative Action" marched on Washington on April 1—the date the Supreme Court heard the case—to support the University of Michigan's admissions policy. They claim the first affirmative action program was actually the college draft deferment that many Euro-American men received during the Vietnam conflict—and that federal programs supporting home ownership are also affirmative action programs that primarily benefit Euro Americans. . . .

The Debate Continues

Whatever decision the Supreme Court makes, disagreements about affirmative action will probably continue. Those who believe in Johnson's hope of equality in education and employment will continue to support the program. Those who fear that they will lose something of their own with the expansion of opportunities for others will continue to denounce it and work for its dismantling. The president's participation in the Supreme Court case will make sure that affirmative action is a political topic of discussion for some time to come.

Meanwhile, as the words fly, people like Marge and her four children, Shirley and her husband, will try to get jobs. Once a month, they will pick up three days' worth of food at the food pantry. And they will continue to believe that if it wasn't for the color of their skin, they would have a job, earn a living, and be building the American Dream.

> *"Affirmative action uses unjust methods to address the wrong problems, and this is why it encounters resentment."*

Affirmative Action Programs Are Unjust

Steven Yates

In the following viewpoint Steven Yates argues that affirmative action programs are an example of how a collectivist conception of social justice harms individuals. White Americans are having their chances at college admissions and employment lowered by affirmative action programs favoring African Americans, even though they bear no individual responsibility for slavery and discrimination against minorities, he maintains. Yates, an adjunct scholar with the Ludwig von Mises Institute and founder of the Worldviews Project, has a PhD in philosophy and has taught the subject full-time for seven years. His published writings include academic articles and reviews and the book *Civil Wrongs: What Went Wrong with Affirmative Action* (1994).

As you read, consider the following questions:
1. What analogy does Yates use to criticize affirmative action?
2. How does the author define *individualism* and *collectivism*?
3. What trends in American society does Yates criticize?

If a white man expresses objections to affirmative action programs, must his motives be racist? . . .

I have written this [viewpoint] for two reasons. One is to express this other side of the affirmative action story. Let's try an analogy.

A Basketball Analogy

Consider a basketball season in which certain teams play by all the familiar rules and others are compelled to play with each player having one arm tied behind his back.

No one, of course, would consider such games fair.

Now suppose someone proposed that for the next several seasons those teams whose players had been untied, were now to play all their games with an arm tied behind their backs, while those who had been tied up, now had both arms free.

Would turnabout be fair play?

Before answering, let's improve the analogy. Let's observe that there has been a complete turnover of players. All those who played in the first set of games have retired. The current players, therefore, are newcomers none of whom were involved with the original practice.

Now let's ask again: would turnabout be fair?

To answer *yes* is to embrace affirmative action. To answer *no* is to reject it, on the grounds that the original perpetrators and beneficiaries of discrimination against blacks are gone (as are their victims), while those forced to sacrifice job opportunities, college admissions, etc., were unborn and so hardly responsible for the wrongs.

Individualism vs. Collectivism

My analogy contains a crucial premise, and it is important to identify it. It focuses on the players as individuals, not as members of collectives. Is it fair or just to penalize the children of a given race for wrongs perpetrated by their remote ancestors?

To say *no* is to take up for an *individualist* model of society, as opposed to a *collectivist* one. The former takes the individual as the most basic unit for analysis; the latter, the group.

Most of human history has been dominated by various sorts of collectivism. It is the easy point of view, the one that divides the human race into tribes. Its logic: you are either part of the tribe or an outcast—probably an enemy. This is why so much of our history is a history of wars and bloodshed.

A Moral Failure

Preferences must . . . be judged a moral failure. Although some individuals have benefited significantly from preferences and a case can be made that preferences have enhanced the economic position of the black middle class, these gains have come at a great moral cost. Put simply, preferences discriminate. They deny opportunities to individuals solely because they are members of a nonpreferred race, gender, or ethnic group. The ambitions and aspirations, the hopes and dreams of individual Americans for themselves and for their families are trampled underfoot not for any wrongs those individuals have committed but for the sake of a bureaucratic effort to counterbalance the supposedly pervasive racism of American society. The penalty for the sins of the society at large is imposed on individuals who themselves are guilty only of being born a member of a nonpreferred group. Individual American citizens who would otherwise enjoy jobs and other opportunities are told that they must be denied in order to tilt the scales of racial justice.

Although preferences are presented as a remedial measure, they in fact create a class of innocent victims of government-imposed discrimination.

Charles T. Canady, *Policy Review*, January/February 1998.

Individualism began its slow rise only in the West, through the gradual convergence of Protestant Christianity, natural-rights political philosophy, and constitutional-republicanism, which saw a written Constitution as encoding the rights of individuals (not groups) that pre-exist government. Individualism is the hard point of view. Escaping tribalism took centuries!

Americans have never been fully consistent individualists. Otherwise the Framers would have gotten rid of slavery at the country's founding. Their not doing so was a blunder of major proportions.

Individualism is nevertheless the superior account of the human condition. There is no collective brain or nervous system. Individuals, not groups, take actions. To the extent that rights are acknowledged as belonging to individuals, societies have prospered. To the extent that human beings have been categorized as groups and moved about by force, societies have stagnated or declined. Marxism, the 20th century's dominant form of collectivism, enslaved and impoverished a third of the human race. The final truth of collectivism is that it doesn't work. Period.

Who Is Responsible for Discrimination?

It therefore behooves us to look at such things as institutional, systemic discrimination to see who is responsible. We see not a collective entity, the "white race," but specific acts of government. These include Supreme Court decisions such as *Plessy v. Ferguson* and also legislation such as 1931's Davis-Bacon Act that made systemic discrimination convenient (it protected unionized workers, and most blacks were not unionized). It also behooves us to look for proximate causes of black disadvantage. Here one sees teen pregnancies, single-parent homes, broken families, substance abuse, and the violent nihilism of the "gangsta rap" culture. Men and women of good conscience—of whatever ethnicity—who would see the plight of black citizens of this country improve must address these real issues, not appeal to that bogey of political correctness, the "legacy of slavery," an institution that hasn't existed for almost 140 years. Once we have done this, I believe we will find that affirmative action uses unjust methods to address the wrong problems, and this is why it encounters resentment and passive resistance.

I mentioned two reasons for writing this [viewpoint]. Everything up till now was the first. The second: I am curious to see whether an ordinary white guy who knows good and well he hasn't reaped some mysterious benefit from being born white can write an article like this and not be demonized (by associates, other commentators, readers) as a covert racist. I have held out for individualism. But with the meteoric rise of political correctness, the complacent acceptance of unlimited immigration, and the dominance of academic ideologies of "diversity" and the "politics of identity," we are now moving backwards towards a society more and more divided into mutually distrustful collectives.

"A debt is owed, and it must be paid in full."

Slavery Reparations Would Promote Social Justice

Manning Marable

More than 135 years after slavery ended in the United States, people are debating whether the descendants of slaves should be compensated for their ancestors' suffering and unpaid labor. In the following viewpoint Manning Marable maintains that African Americans deserve such reparations from the federal government and corporations who profited from slavery. He argues that while white Americans alive today are not guilty of enslaving anyone, they continue to benefit from slavery's legacy. He further argues that white Americans bear a collective responsibility for slavery and the continuing mistreatment of African Americans. Marable is a professor of African American studies at Columbia University and the author of the numerous books on race and class in the United States, including *Beyond Black and White: Race in America's Past, Present, and Future* and *How Capitalism Underdeveloped Black America.*

As you read, consider the following questions:
1. What does the American public believe about slavery reparations, according to Marable?
2. What are some of the conservative arguments against reparations that the author attempts to rebut?
3. What is the greatest challenge facing the reparations movement, according to Marable?

Throughout this year [2002], the black reparations debate has become widely known, and it continued to attract increased national and international attention. In February 2002, CNN and *USA Today* commissioned the Gallup organization to conduct a national poll to assess public opinion on the issue. The results seemed to directly mirror the nation's parallel racial universes that are reproduced by structural racism.

When asked whether "corporations that made profits from slavery should apologize to black Americans who are descendants of slaves," 68 percent of African Americans responded affirmatively, with 23 percent opposed, while 62 percent of all whites rejected the call for an apology, with only 34 percent supporting it.

On the question of financial compensation, however, whites closed ranks around their racial privileges. When asked whether corporations benefiting from slave exploitation should "make cash payments to black Americans who are the descendants of slaves," 84 percent of all whites responded negatively, with only 11 percent supporting payments. A clear majority of African Americans polled, by contrast, endorsed corporate restitution payments, by a 57 to 35 percent margin, with 8 percent expressing no opinion.

When asked if the government should grant "cash payments" to blacks, nine out of ten white Americans rejected the proposal, while a strong majority of blacks favored it, by 55 to 37 percent. . . .

Answering Arguments

It was inevitable that as the demand for reparations achieved majority support among African Americans, black conservatives would be trotted out to defend the preservation of white power and privilege. The premier black apologist for the worst policies of the Reagan administration in the black community, economist Thomas Sowell, declared that "the first thing to understand about the issue of reparations is that no money is going to be paid."

Sowell argued that the reparations cause was nothing more than an elaborate plot by black "demagogues," because "they are demanding something they know they are not going to get. But if we start operating on the principle that people alive today are responsible for what their ancestors did in centuries past, we will be adopting a principle that can tear any society apart, especially a multiethnic society like the United States."

Conservative economist Walter Williams seconded Sowell's objections, observing that "the problem, of course, is both slaves as well as their owners are all dead. What moral principle justifies forcing a white of today to pay a black of today for what a white of yesteryear did to a black of yesteryear?". . .

Younger black neoconservatives such as John McWhorter pointed out that even if the reparations movement succeeded in its efforts to create a national "slavery fund" to provide new resources to impoverished black communities, it would only reproduce the unequal structures of black dependency. "The reparation crowd's move from individual checks to a general fund will allow community-wide assistance," McWhorter admitted, "but this model has done nothing for forty years now. Who would get the money? For what purpose?"

The black conservatives' criticisms and complaints can easily be addressed. First, there is a crucial difference between "guilt" and "responsibility." White Americans who are alive today are not guilty of enslaving anyone, in the legal definition of the term. Most white Americans below the age of fifty played no role in directly supporting Jim Crow segregation and are not guilty of overt acts to block the integration of public accommodations and schools.

But white Americans, as a group, continue to be the direct beneficiaries of the legal apparatuses of white supremacy, carried out by the full weight of America's legal, political, and economic institutions. The consequences of state-sponsored racial inequality created a mountain of historically constructed, accumulated disadvantage for African Americans as a group.

Racism's Living Legacy

The living legacy of that racialized, accumulated disadvantage can easily be measured by looking at the gross racial deficits that segment Americans by race, in their life expectancies and in their unequal access to home ownership, business development, and quality education. The U.S. government, for nearly two centuries, established the legal parameters for corporations to carry out blatantly discriminatory policies and practices.

Reparations and Social Justice

If we think of reparations as part of a broad strategy to radically transform society—redistributing wealth, creating a democratic and caring public culture, exposing the ways capitalism and slavery produced massive inequality—then the ongoing struggle for reparations holds enormous promise for revitalizing movements for social justice. . . .

The argument for reparations . . . shows how more than two centuries of U.S. policy facilitated accumulation among white property owners while further impoverishing African Americans. Thus federal assistance to black people in any form is not a gift but a down payment for centuries of unpaid labor, violence, and exploitation.

Robin D.G. Kelley, *Against the Current*, January/February 2003.

Consequently, it is insufficient for us to simply say that once the Jim Crow laws were changed, the state's responsibility to redress those victimized by discriminatory public policies ended. The U.S. government and the various state governments that created and perpetuated legal racial disparities are "responsible" for compensating the victims and their descendants. As citizens of this country, whites must bear the financial burden of the crimes against humanity that were carried out by their own government.

Another way of thinking about this is to point to the fiscal mismanagement and repressive social policies of the Reagan administration two decades ago. Billions of dollars of tax money paid by blacks and whites alike were allocated to the military industrial complex to finance global military interventions and a nuclear arms race. The vast majority of African Americans strongly opposed these reactionary policies.

We were not "guilty" of participating in the decisions to carry out such policies. Yet, as citizens, we are "responsible" for paying to finance Reagan's disastrous militarism, which left the country deeply in debt. We have an obligation under law to pay taxes. Thus, all citizens of the United States have the same "responsibility" to compensate members of their own society that were deliberately stigmatized by legal racism. Individual "guilt" or "innocence" is therefore irrelevant.

America's version of legal apartheid created the conditions of white privilege and black subordination that we see all around us every day. A debt is owed, and it must be paid in full. . . .

What reparations does is to force whites to acknowledge the brutal reality of our common history, something white society generally has refused to do. It provides a historically-grounded explanation for the continuing burden of racial oppression: the unequal distribution of economic resources, land, and access to opportunities for social development, which was sanctioned by the federal government.

Consequently it is that same government that bears the responsibility of compensating those citizens and their descendants to whom constitutional rights were denied. Affirmative action was essentially "paycheck equality," in the words of political scientist Ronald Walters; it created millions of job opportunities, bud did relatively little to transfer wealth from one racial group to another.

One-third of all African-American households today has a negative net wealth. The average black household's wealth is less than 15 percent of the typical white household's. Most of our people are trapped in an almost bottomless economic pit from which there will be no escape—unless we change our political demands and strategy from liberal integrationism to a restructuring of economic resources, and the elimination of structural deficits that separate blacks and whites into unequal racial universes.

From Handout to Payback

"Reparations" transforms the dynamics of the national racial discourse, moving from "handouts" to "paybacks." It parallels a global movement by people of African descent and other Third World people to renegotiate debt and to demand compensation for slavery, colonialism, and apartheid. . . .

"Economic reparations" could take a variety of forms, any of which could be practically implemented. I favor the establishment of a reparations social fund that would channel federal, state, and/or corporate funds for investment in nonprofit, community-based organizations, economic empowerment zones in areas with high rates of unemployment, and grants or interest-free loans for blacks to purchase homes or to start businesses in economically depressed neighborhoods.

Lasting Repercussions

In response to our call [for black reparations], individual Americans need not feel defensive or under attack. No one holds any living person responsible for slavery or the later century-plus of legal relegation of blacks to substandard education, exclusion from home ownership via restrictive covenants and redlining, or any of the myriad mechanisms for pushing blacks to the back of the line. Nonetheless, we must all, as a nation, ponder the repercussions of those acts.

Randall Robinson, *Nation*, March 13, 2000.

However, there are other approaches to the reconstruction of black economic opportunity. Sociologist Dalton Conley has suggested the processing of "individual checks via the tax system, like a refundable slavery tax credit." Major corporations and banks that were "unjustly enriched" by either slave labor or by Jim Crow–era discriminatory policies against African Americans could set aside a portion of future profits in a trust fund to financially compensate their victims and their descendants.

Universities whose endowments were based on the slave trade or on slave labor and/or companies that were unjustly enriched by racial segregation laws could create scholarship funds to give greater access to African-American students.

Challenges to the Reparations Movement

It would be dangerous and foolish for the proponents of reparations to quarrel among themselves over the best approach for implementation at this time. Over a generation ago, there were numerous divisions within the Civil Rights Movement, separating leaders and rival organizations. They all agreed on the general goal, the abolition of legal racial segregation, but espoused very different ways and tactics to get there. The same model should be applied to reparations.

Any effort to impose rigid ideological or organizational conformity on this diverse and growing popular movement will only serve to disrupt and destroy it.

As I have written previously, the greatest challenge in the national debate over African-American reparations is in convincing black people, not whites, that we can actually win. The greatest struggle of the oppressed is always against their own weaknesses, doubts, and fears. The reparations demand is most liberating because it has the potential for transforming how black people see themselves, and our own history.

*"Paying the descendants of slaves a
monetary settlement today, more than 135
years after slavery ended, will do nothing."*

Slavery Reparations Would Not Promote Social Justice

Linda Chavez

Linda Chavez is a columnist and president of the Center for
Equal Opportunity. Her writings include the book *An Unlikely Conservative: The Transformation of an Ex-Liberal (or How
I Became the Most Hated Hispanic in America)*. In the viewpoint
that follows, she concedes that slavery was an unjust chapter
in American history, and that slaves should have been compensated immediately after slavery was abolished. But she
goes on to assert that financial reparations for the descendants of American slaves are not the way to redress slavery or
attain justice for African Americans. It is impossible to determine who should make or receive such payments more than
a century after slavery's demise, Chavez maintains.

As you read, consider the following questions:
1. What is the real impetus behind the movement for
   reparations, according to Chavez?
2. How have black Americans been unjustly treated in the
   past, according to the author?
3. What alternative to "writing a check" does Chavez
   propose for redressing the past injustices of slavery?

If it were possible to wipe out the legacy of slavery by writing a big, fat check, I'd be all for it. Who wouldn't be in favor of a simple solution to the problems that plague much of the African American community in America today—especially since all of us are affected, not just blacks? Imagine, a one-time payment that would solve family breakdown, poverty and homicide among young, black males. But there are no easy solutions, and the payment of reparations to the descendants of slaves certainly isn't the answer. It's just more of the same liberal cure-all: Let government redistribute money from one group to try to solve the problems of another.

The reparations movement got a big boost this week [May 30, 2001] when one of America's most distinguished newspapers, the *Philadelphia Inquirer*, endorsed the concept in an editorial. But the real impetus behind the reparations campaign is the grievance industry—that group of professional guilt-mongers who hope to enrich themselves by claiming to represent the downtrodden.

An Indelible Stain

There is no question that slavery indelibly stains American history. How is it that a nation founded on the principle that all men are created equal could perpetuate a system in which some men owned others, like mere chattel? But 140,000 Union soldiers died to expiate slavery, so to suggest that no white Americans ever suffered for the sins of slavery is simply wrong.

Still, slaves should have been compensated immediately after the Civil War for the great harm they endured. Congress promised, then failed to deliver, 40 acres and a mule to every former slave. The course of American history might well have been different had all the reforms promised to the Freedmen's Bureau been enacted. As it was, of the post-Civil War Amendments passed by Congress to right the wrongs of American slavery, only the 13th Amendment, which abolished slavery, was fully implemented. The 14th Amendment, which guaranteed equal protection of the laws, and the 15th Amendment, which guaranteed blacks the right to vote, were universally ignored in the Deep South and throughout much of the nation for more than 100 years after they were adopted.

Asay. © 2002 by Creators Syndicate, Inc. Reproduced by permission.

The failure to do what was right at the time has cost this country greatly. As Gunnar Myrdahl wrote more than 50 years ago in his great treatise on America's race problems, *American Dilemma*, virtually all of the social problems encountered in the black community can be traced back to slavery and the era of Jim Crow laws, which deprived blacks of their most basic rights. But the question is, how do you solve those problems now?

Payment Raises Questions

Paying the descendants of slaves a monetary settlement today, more than 135 years after slavery ended, will do nothing. Nor is it possible to determine who should receive payments and who should pay them. Some African Americans are descended from persons who came to the United States long after slavery was abolished, including the thousands of Haitians, Dominicans and other Caribbean immigrants of the last 30 years. These person's ancestors may have been slaves in their native land, but should the United States have to pay for the sins of all slave-owning nations?

More importantly, why should Americans whose ancestors did not benefit from slavery, or who may not even have lived in the United States at the time slavery existed, have to pay for these sins? Indeed it is a new variation on punishing the sons for the sins of the fathers to insist that all whites who live in the United States today must compensate all blacks who happen to live here now. Most whites are not descended from slave-owners. Nor are they the beneficiaries of ill-begotten gains from slavery, which hampered—not helped—the early American economy. The South remained an economic backwater from the 19th century until the modern civil rights era, in large part because the region failed to take advantage of its best resource: human capital. Discrimination on the basis of race is bad business, and the South failed to thrive until it put aside officially-sanctioned racism.

Slavery will always remain America's Original Sin. But the best way to absolve ourselves is not by writing a check but by resolving never again to treat another human being as less than our equal because of the color of his skin.

Periodical Bibliography

The following articles have been selected to supplement the diverse views presented in this chapter.

Michael Bérubé	"And Justice for All," *Nation*, January 24, 2005.
David L. Chappell	"If Affirmative Action Fails . . . What Then?" *New York Times*, May 8, 2004.
Maria Clara Dias	"Affirmative Action and Social Justice," *Connecticut Law Review*, Spring 2004.
Mark Edmundson	"Civil Disobedience Against Affirmative Action," *New York Times Magazine*, December 14, 2003.
William P. Hoar	"Benign Discrimination?" *New American*, May 5, 2003.
Wilbert Jenkins	"Why We Must Retain Affirmative Action," *USA Today*, September 1999.
John Leo	"Enslaved to the Past," *U.S. News & World Report*, April 15, 2002.
Manning Marable	"An Idea Whose Time Has Come . . . Whites Have an Obligation to Recognize Slavery's Legacy," *Newsweek*, August 27, 2001.
Chris Matthews	"White Blindness," *San Francisco Chronicle*, July 15, 2001.
Nation	"Beyond Black, White, and Brown," May 3, 2004.
Rene A. Redwood	"I'm an Affirmative-Action Baby and Proud! Affirmative Action Allows Everyone a Fair Chance," *Essence*, January 1999.
Randall Robinson	"America's Debt to Blacks," *Nation*, March 13, 2000.
Carol M. Swain	"Do Blacks Deserve a National Apology? Should Today's Citizenry Be Held Morally and Financially Accountable for the Misdeeds of America's Forefathers?" *USA Today*, January 2004.
Stuart Taylor Jr.	"Do African-Americans Really Want Racial Preferences?" *National Journal*, December 21, 2002.

Ronald Walters   "Reparations for Slavery? Let's Resolve the Inequity," *World & I*, April 2000.

Jack White   "Don't Waste Your Breath: The Fight for Slave Reparations Is a Morally Just but Totally Hopeless Cause," *Time*, April 2, 2001.

Sheryl J. Willert   "Affirmative Action: The Benefits of Diversity," *National Law Journal*, September 8, 2003.

CHAPTER 3

What Policies Would Promote Social Justice for Women?

Chapter Preface

A principle many people would concede as just is the idea of "equal pay for equal work." The idea that a woman would be paid less for doing the same job as a man strikes many people as fundamentally unfair. Indeed, the federal government has made this kind of discrimination illegal by passing the 1963 Equal Pay Act, which prohibits unequal pay for equal or "substantially equal" work performed by men and women.

However, despite the passage of the 1963 law and the widespread growth and acceptance of women in the workplace in the decades that followed, there remains a significant pay gap between what men and women earn in the American workplace. Census Bureau statistics show that in 2003, women earned seventy-six cents on average for every dollar men earned (this was up from fifty-nine cents in 1963, but down one cent from 2002). The National Committee on Pay Equity (NCPE), a coalition of civil rights and labor organizations, blames the wage gap on a society that segregates women into a "pink-collar ghetto" of low-paying occupations. "More than half of all women workers hold sales, clerical and service jobs," states the NCPE. The coalition asserts: "Studies show that the more an occupation is dominated by women or people of color, the less it pays. Part of the wage gap results from differences in education, experience or time in the workforce. But a significant portion cannot be explained by any of those factors; it is attributable to discrimination." The NCPE and others have supported government laws to regulate wages and make them equal between men and women.

However, not everyone agrees that the statistical differences between men's and women's pay proves discrimination or an unjust society. Yale economics professor Jennefer Roback argues, "Many of the factors that contribute to the earnings gap are the result of personal choices made by women themselves, not decisions thrust on them by bosses." These personal choices, Roback and others argue, include the decision to take time off to have children (thus forgoing the seniority and experience male employees accrue), or seeking part-time work or flexible hours in order to better care for their children. Roback is one of many who conclude that the difference in men's and women's earnings is not proof of discrimination, and that the wage gap is not something that can or should be corrected by government regulation.

The pay gap between men and women continues to spark debate. The viewpoints in this chapter examine the causes of the gender pay gap and explore other issues relating to how women are treated in American society.

"The average woman . . . will lose $523,000 in her lifetime due to unequal pay."

Women Earn Less than Men Due to Gender Discrimination

Joel Wendland

Although women have made some progress in recent decades in attaining economic equality with men, women's pay still averages roughly three-quarters of men's pay, writes Joel Wendland in the following viewpoint. He disputes the argument that a "reverse gender gap" advantageous to women is emerging in American society. Women still earn less and have smaller savings and pension benefits than men on average, while women with children are especially hurt by gender inequality. Wendland is managing editor of *Political Affairs*, a publication of the Communist Party USA.

As you read, consider the following questions:
1. What "new gender gap" does Wendland seek to debunk?
2. What is the "price of motherhood" that women must cope with, according to the author?
3. Why are men hurt as well as women by wage inequality, according to Wendland?

"Boys are becoming the second sex" proclaimed *Business Week* last May [2003] in a cover story titled "The New Gender Gap." *Business Week's* article appeared as part of a spate of articles and television news segments on the subject of increased educational opportunities for women. The basics of the story are that in the education system, teachers have become so conscious of catering to the needs of girls and young women that boys are being left behind. Boys, they say, are being punished for "boyish" behavior. They are being put more often into special education programs or disciplinary classes, and the outcome is that boys have a negative educational experience. This trend translates into poorer high school performances and perhaps college as well.

According to statistics offered by *Business Week*, 57 percent of all new bachelor's degrees and 58 percent of master's degrees are awarded to women. This "education grab," according to the article, was the source of the "new gender gap." Though, the article did hint that even with the new trend in the numbers, women still had some ways to go in order to catch up after 350 years of being almost entirely excluded from the university.

Most observers of this situation will find such an article perplexing. Certainly most women will likely be skeptical of its major argument. That this "reverse gender gap" argument exists, however, is not surprising. Like its cousins in other areas of social life (reverse discrimination or reverse class warfare), it is being generated primarily by the ultra-right. The purpose is to stifle the struggle for equality by implying (or stating directly) that the gains made by women through struggle over the last 40 years have gone too far and have detrimentally affected society.

Some in this camp go so far as to suggest that women who demand equality are out to hurt men. At worst, it demonstrates that the right wants to twist the outcome of social progress to divide us. They say that a struggle between men and women for social goods is the fundamental source of social conflict and that women are winning—a situation that, for some, means reversed gender inequality and for others goes against natural laws of male supremacy invoked by God.

Distorted Reality

Any way you look at it, however, this picture is a distortion of reality. So what does the real gender gap look like?

Barbara Gault, director of research at ,the Institute for Women's Policy Research, recently told *Women'sWallStreet. com* that there are several explanations for and holes in the current data on the educational experiences of men and women. First, high-paying occupations that do not require college degrees, such as skilled trades, are still male dominated. Second, women need a college degree in order to earn roughly what men do with only high school diplomas, giving them stronger motives to make a special effort to obtain financial security. Third, among African Americans, where the difference between women and men earning college degrees is the widest among all racial or ethnic groups, it is clear that institutional racism directed at African American men plays a large role in keeping them out of college. Fourth, in the crucial field of information technology, women continue to earn only about one-third of the degrees awarded and get only about one-third of the jobs available. Finally, men continue to outpace women in completing doctoral and professional degrees (81 women for every 100 men). resulting in continued male dominance in corporate board rooms, the seats of political power, the highest positions in universities, etc.

The successes of the women's equality movement, progressive changes in attitudes about roles women can have and the implementation of affirmative action policies (which benefited women as a whole most) have had a tremendous positive impact on the access women have had in education. Just 30 years ago, women earned advanced or professional degrees at a rate of only 23 women per 100 men. In other arenas, such as the workforce or the political field, the gender gap, in sheer numbers, has largely narrowed. But the numbers still don't paint the whole picture.

While higher education is a major factor in gaining financial security, it is something that is only available to about one-fifth of the adult population. So for the vast majority of women, this supposed "new gender gap" means absolutely nothing. Other data on the condition of women's economic security paint another picture altogether. About eight of ten retired women are not eligible for pension benefits. When retired women do get a pension, it is typically far less than retired men get. Fifty percent of women who receive pension benefits get only about 60 cents for every dollar of male pensioners. On the average, retired women depend on Social Security for 71 percent of their income, and about 25 percent of retired women rely solely on Social Security for their income.

The Wage Gap Reflects Sex Discrimination

The wage gap cannot be dismissed as the result of "women's choices" in career and family matters. In fact, recent authoritative studies show that even when all relevant career and family attributes are taken into account, there is still a significant, unexplained gap in men's and women's earnings. Thus, even when women make the same career choices as men and work the same hours, they still earn less.

A 2003 study by U.S. Government Accounting Office found that, even when all the key factors that influence earnings are controlled for—demographic factors such as marital status, race, number and age of children, and income, as well as work patterns such as years of work, hours worked, and job tenure—women still earned, on average, only 80% of what men earned in 2000. That is, 20% of the pay gap between women and men could not be explained or justified.

National Women's Law Center, April 2004.

In the workforce, women's pay averages only 76 percent of men's pay (at a cost of about $200 billion for working families annually). A report produced by the General Accounting Office last October [2003] shows that since 1983, the wage differential has actually increased. 60 percent of all women earn less than $25,000 annually. Women are one-third more likely to live below the poverty level. Black women and Latinas are between two and three times more likely to live below the poverty line than men are. For women of color, facing the double oppression of racism and sexism, pay losses are even greater: 64 cents on the dollar at a loss of about $210 a week. The average woman, according to the AFL-CIO, will lose $523,000 in her lifetime due to unequal pay.

The Price of Motherhood

Even more costly to women, is the "price of motherhood," as journalist Ann Crittenden argues in her recent book of that title. In almost every case, women lose income, jobs, job experience and retirement income (while work hours increase) when they decide to have children. With some slight improvements, women remain the primary caregiver in nearly every family. For many mothers, single or married, the economic inequalities described above are exacerbated. For married women, dependence on men is heightened and the threat of economic hardship enforces interpersonal inequality and conflict. Divorced mothers and their children have among the highest rates of poverty of any demographic.

Crittenden argues that unless other sources of financial support for motherhood are made available institutionalized inequality will persist. She suggests retirement benefits for mothers, public funding for day care and health care for children and their caregivers, salaries for primary caregivers, expanded public education for pre-school children, equalized social security for spouses, increased financial contributions from husbands and fathers, increased educational and support resources for parents and equalization of living standards for divorced parents.

Men Hurt Too

As for the fallacy of female supremacy, the gains made by women through struggle and implementation of policies such as affirmative action point to the necessity of broader systematic change. But if female supremacy is a fallacy, does this mean that men go unhurt by gender inequalities? No. Men and boys are hurt when their families suffer because pay inequity causes their mothers, grandmothers, sisters and aunts to lose income, get fired, face hiring discrimination, are refused pensions, don't have equal Social Security benefits, lose out on promotions or have limited access to higher education. Additionally, if the average woman loses $523,000 in income in her life, does this mean that the average man is enriched by $523,000 in his lifetime? If pay inequity costs women $200 billion yearly, does this mean that men are enriched by $200 billion? The answer is no. These billions are savings in labor costs to employers. Employers enjoy the profits of male supremacy and gendered divisions among working people. So it makes sense that the right tries to portray the benefits of progressive social change toward equality as bad. It cuts into their bottom line.

| "The 'wage gap' is not so much about
employers discriminating against women
as about women making discriminating
choices in the labor market."

Women Do Not Earn Less than Men Due to Gender Discrimination

Denise Venable

Some observers have pointed to the persistent gap between what men and women earn in the workplace as evidence of unjust gender discrimination in American society. In the viewpoint that follows, Denise Venable argues that the so-called wage gap between men and women is not as serious a problem as is sometimes reported. She contends that much of the difference between what women and men earn stems from the individual choices women make rather than from gender. Women often opt for flexibility in their jobs over higher-earning positions, she points out. Denise Venable is a research assistant for the National Center for Policy Analysis, a public policy research organization that promotes private alternatives to government regulation.

As you read, consider the following questions:
1. What is the wage gap among childless workers aged twenty-seven to thirty-three, according to Venable?
2. What lifestyle choices have affected what women earn in the workplace, according to the author?
3. Has the wage gap between the two sexes been growing or shrinking, according to Venable?

Tuesday, April 16, 2002, is Equal Pay Day—the day on which many organizations protest wage discrimination between men and women. According to the U.S. Bureau of Labor Statistics, the median income for all women is about three-quarters that of men, although the results vary significantly among demographic groups. Feminist organizations and some politicians point to these statistics as evidence of the United States as a patriarchal society that discriminates against women. But a closer examination leads to a different conclusion.

The Good News. When women behave in the workplace as men do, the wage gap between them is small. June O'Neill, former director of the Congressional Budget Office, found that among people ages 27 to 33 who have never had a child, women's earnings approach 98 percent of men's. Women who hold positions and have skills and experience similar to those of men face wage disparities of less than 10 percent, and many are within a couple of points. Claims of unequal pay almost always involve comparing apples and oranges.

Lifestyle Choices. Women make different choices, and those choices affect how they work. Women often place more importance on their relationships—caring for children, parents, spouses, etc.—than on their careers. A study by the Center for Policy Alternatives and Lifetime television found that 71 percent of women prefer jobs with more flexibility and benefits than jobs with higher wages, and nearly 85 percent of women offered flexible work arrangements by their employers have taken advantage of this opportunity.

Entry and Exit from the Job Market. Women are more likely to enter and leave the workforce to raise children, take care of elderly parents or move with their families. Working mothers are nearly twice as likely to take time off to care for their children as are working fathers in dual-earner couples. Yet time out of the workforce is an enormous obstacle to building an attractive resume and working up the corporate ladder. Women 25 years of age and over have been with their current employer 4.4 years, on average, compared to 5.0 years for men. Data from the National Longitudinal Survey reveal that women between the ages of 18 and 34 have been out of the labor force 27 percent of the time, in contrast to

11 percent for men. Women ages 45 to 54 who have recently re-entered the workforce after a five- or 10-year break are competing against men who have had 20 years of continuous experience.

Part-Time Work. Women are also more likely to work part-time. In 2000, one-quarter of all women employees worked part-time, compared to less than 10 percent of men. Nearly 85 percent of those who worked part-time did so for non-economic reasons; e.g., to spend more time with the family or to further their education. In general, married women would prefer part-time work at a rate of 5 to 1 over married men.

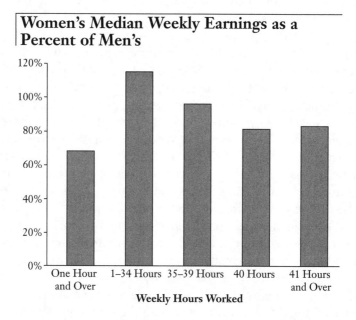

Women's Median Weekly Earnings as a Percent of Men's

Weekly Hours Worked

"Highlights of Women's Earnings in 2000," Report 952, U.S. Department of Labor, Bureau of Labor Statistics, August 2001.

While part-time work usually increases flexibility, the part-time worker loses out on promotions and pay increases. Part-time work also tends to mean lower hourly pay. Shorter labor stints and part-time work contribute to the probability of working for the minimum wage. Nearly two-thirds of minimum wage earners are women.

However, women's wages hold up quite well to men's wages when comparing specific job categories. Among adults working between one and 34 hours a week, women's earnings are 115 percent of men's. Among part-time workers who have never married, and who thus confront fewer outside factors likely to affect earnings, women earn slightly more than men. These statistics suggest that skill level, tenure and working hours—not gender—determine wages.

Occupational Choices. Beyond work behavior, women gravitate to sectors of the economy that compensate workers at lower levels. While women hold 53 percent of all professional jobs in the United States, they hold only 28 percent of jobs in professions averaging $40,000 or more in annual compensation. For example, fewer women have chosen to enter such technical fields as computer sciences, math and science teaching, medicine, law and engineering. In 1998, women earned only 26.7 percent of computer science degrees.

Closing the Gap. Despite all these factors, the gap between men and women's wages has been closing. . . . Over the last 20 years women's earnings have jumped at least 12 percentage points relative to men's earnings, closing the wage differential at every level of education. A change in women's work expectations also has tended to close the gap. Until the 1970s, a minority of women expected to work after marriage. Today, almost 75 percent of young women expect to be working at age 35.

Changing work expectations are an apparent cause of women's increased focus on education, and the enrollment of women in higher education has grown much faster than that of men. Women were awarded more than 50 percent of associate's, bachelor's and master's degrees in the 1990s. Women currently earn more than 40 percent of Ph.D.s, medical and law degrees.

The narrowing of the gender wage gap approximately one percentage point a year since 1980 is particularly significant, since during the 1980s and '90s the overall wage level rose little and the wage inequality between skilled and unskilled workers grew. Without enhanced skills, women's wages likely would have fallen further behind men's. However, market pressures have helped to generate corrective mechanisms, and as the costs of denying employment to women mounted, prejudices were set aside.

Conclusion. Women's work-life patterns and their occupational preferences are significant factors in determining wages. Rather than being "funneled" into low-wage, low-prestige and part-time positions, women often choose these occupations because of the flexibility they offer. After adjusting for these factors, scholars find that the difference between men's and women's earnings is very narrow.

Those who still cite women's 76 cents for every male dollar as evidence of sexism fail to take into account the underlying role of personal choice. The "wage gap" is not so much about employers discriminating against women as about women making discriminating choices in the labor market.

"It's time to get serious about equal pay."

Comparable Worth Policies Promote Social Justice

Heather Boushey

Heather Boushey is an economist for the Center for Economic and Policy Research, a nonprofit organization that promotes democratic debate on social and economic issues. She has written numerous articles and books about U.S. labor markets and social policy issues, including *Hardships in America: The Real Story of Working Families*. In the following viewpoint she argues that the continuing pay gap between what men and women earn in the workplace is due in part to the segregation of men and women into different job categories. She claims that jobs traditionally dominated by women are poorly paid compared with occupations with similar skills and education that are held mostly by men. She calls for government legislation that would mandate equal pay for jobs with comparable responsibilities and skills—a policy known as "comparable worth."

As you read, consider the following questions:

1. Why did the pay gap between men and women fall in the 1980s, according to Boushey?
2. Why have affirmative action programs and antidiscrimination laws only partially succeeded in closing the gender wage gap, according to the author?
3. How would comparable worth laws reduce poverty, according to Boushey?

I magine working without pay all day Monday and just before your Tuesday morning coffee break. Sounds ridiculous, right?

Unfortunately, it's the reality for many women.

Because women working full-time earn, on average, 80
cents for every dollar earned by men, they work longer
hours for the same paycheck. That's why each year Equal
Pay Day is observed on a Tuesday (April 3 this year [2001]).
It is meant to promote renewed focus on the sharp gender
inequality that persists in our workplaces today.

The Pay Gap

During the 1980s, the pay gap narrowed not because women
made progress, but because men's wages fell dramatically.
Even as the economy heated up during the 1990s and women's
college attendance and completion rates surpassed men's, the
pay gap held steady. Among full-time, full-year workers, the
gap peaked at 81 percent in 1993 and has hovered around that
level ever since.

This pay gap is not due to differences in the skills and attributes that women and men bring to the labor market. The
gap is the same for full-time workers who went to college as
for those who didn't.

Several policies have helped to close the wage gap as
women and people of color moved into higher-paying jobs
historically open only to white men.

The Equal Pay Act, passed in 1963, prohibits employers
from paying a woman less than a man for doing the same job.
The following year, Title VII of the Civil Rights Act expanded
the scope of anti-discrimination protections to hiring, firing,
promotion, and most other conditions of employment.

Affirmative Action was designed to go a step further, requiring government contractors and other employers to set
formal goals to remedy the past underrepresentation of
women and minority employees.

But it's now clear that they're not enough to close the gap
completely.

It remains in part because of the high degree of segregation
of women and men into different types of jobs. As a result, another policy approach, comparable worth, has drawn increased

attention as a possible means for eliminating the wage penalty for working in a predominantly female occupation.

Occupations that have been historically dominated by women are often poorly paid compared to occupations that are dominated by men and that require comparable levels of skill and education—nursing, which requires high levels of education and certification, yet is underpaid—is one example.

One Man's Story

Perhaps the most dramatic argument for comparable worth, . . . was made by a man. . . . Milt Tedrow [was] a licensed practical nurse [LPN] at Eastern State Hospital in Spokane. Approaching retirement and realizing that his "woman's" job wouldn't give him much of a pension, Tedrow switched to carpentry at the same hospital. To qualify as an LPN he had needed at least four years of experience, four quarters of schooling, and a license. As a carpenter, he was self-taught, had no paid work experience, and had no need of a license. And yet when he transferred from the top of the LPN wage scale to the bottom of the carpenter's his salary jumped more than $200 a month— from $1,614 to $1,826. Why, Tedrow wondered at the time, does the state resent "paying people decently who are taking care of people's bodies, when they'd pay a lot for someone fixing cars or plumbing"?

Naomi Barko, *American Prospect*, June 19–July 3, 2000.

The Fair Pay Act, introduced today [April 8, 2001] by Eleanor Holmes-Norton in the House and Tom Harkin in the Senate, is comparable-worth legislation requiring that firms give equal pay to workers that have jobs with comparable skill requirements and responsibilities. Similar legislation has been introduced in 28 states and is pending in another three [as of 2001].

The proposed comparable-worth legislation could reduce the wage gap and help low-wage workers without creating an excessive burden for employers.

The Paycheck Fairness Act, a pending bill co-sponsored by Tom Daschle in the Senate and Rosa DeLauro in the House, would amend the Fair Labor Standards Act to eliminate discrimination that leads to pay inequities by enhancing enforcement of equal pay requirements.[1]

Millions of women across the United States work two jobs: mother and breadwinner. As mothers increasingly are working outside the home, such measures are needed now more than ever to help women balance work and family.

Equitable pay for married women would mean that their family incomes would rise by nearly six percent, and fewer families would live in poverty. For single working mothers, family incomes would increase by nearly 17 percent, and poverty rates for their families would be cut in half, from 25.3 percent to 12.6 percent.

Given how hard women work, the pay gap isn't just too big—it's ridiculous. It's time to get serious about equal pay.

1. Neither the Fair Play Act nor the Paycheck Fairness Act had become law as of 2004.

"Comparable worth is a poor solution to a nonexistent problem."

Comparable Worth Policies Do Not Promote Social Justice

Rebecca A. Thacker and Joshua C. Hall

Rebecca A. Thacker is a professor of management at Ohio University. Joshua C. Hall is the director of research at the Buckeye Institute, an independent research institute that analyzes state and local programs in the state of Ohio. In the viewpoint that follows, they criticize comparable worth legislation, arguing that its premise—that women earn less than men due to historical and ongoing sexual discrimination—is flawed. The wage gap between men and women vanishes when variables such as work history and education are taken into account, they contend. Government intervention mandating that companies give equal pay to workers who have jobs with like responsibilities and requirements ignores the role that supply and demand plays in setting wages and may lead to shortages of workers in some jobs, Thacker and Hall maintain.

As you read, consider the following questions:

1. What happened in Minnesota following the passage of comparable worth legislation, according to Thacker and Hall?
2. What variables influence the wages people earn, according to the authors?
3. What evidence of women's progress do Thacker and Hall cite?

In 1963, John F. Kennedy signed the Equal Pay Act into law. The Equal Pay Act made it illegal for employers to pay unequal wages to men and women employed in the same job with the same characteristics, such as longevity and performance. At the time of its passage, the median woman earned 58 percent of what the median man earned.

Forty years later, according to the National Committee on Pay Equity, the median woman earns 75 percent of what the median man earns. This oft-cited statistic is the reasoning behind policy proposals that seek to go beyond "equal pay for equal work," such as "comparable worth" or "paycheck fairness."

The Premise Behind Comparable Worth

The premise underlying comparable worth and paycheck fairness is that female-dominated jobs are paid less than male-dominated jobs simply because they are female dominated. Comparable worth advocates argue that wages in female-dominated professions are lower because of sexual discrimination, both historical and ongoing, and government intervention is needed to remedy this imbalance until the gap between the wages of men and women is eliminated.

Comparable worth proponents deny that supply and demand set wages in the labor market. From their perspective, businesses don't really pay employees in female-dominated industries what they are "worth" to the business. Outside "experts" therefore must be appointed, by law, to tell them what various employees are "worth" to them.

If the experts decide that the job of cleaning personnel is comparable to the job of receptionist, by law the employer must pay the janitor the same as the receptionist. In practice, this tends to lead to shortages, as wages no longer reflect supply and demand in the marketplace.

In Minnesota, for example, nurse shortages arose in many cities after the passage of comparable worth legislation. Many job evaluation systems determined that nurses were paid more than they were "worth." This occurred despite already existing nurse shortages that would normally indicate the need to *raise* wages. The subsequent decline in nurses' compensation led to an even greater shortage of nurses illustrating perfectly the danger of ignoring supply and demand in setting wage rates.

Comparable Worth Is Not a Cure-All

Comparable worth is not a cure-all. Since comparable worth typically addresses wage gaps within a single workplace, it does not help workers whose employers pay everyone the minimum wage. Without strong unions, comparable worth won't get very far even if new legislation were enacted; for one thing, it is unions that are most likely to be able to fund the expensive litigation necessary to force companies to revise their pay scales. At a deeper level, existing comparable-worth policies largely accept how the U.S. economic system has typically rewarded different job factors. It is one thing to even out pay inequities between jobs that rate the same on existing job-evaluation instruments. It would be far more radical to rebuild our notions of fair compensation in a way that values the skills of caring, communication, and responsibility for people's emotional well-being that are critical to many female-dominated occupations.

Amy Gluckman, *Dollars & Sense*, September/October 2002.

A comparison of wage rates between men and women is a dubious measure of discrimination anyway, and should not be used to make public policy. The oft-cited statistic that women make just 75 percent of what men make is based on the wages of the *median* man and woman.

Other Variables

The median is an aggregate, a measure of central tendency. As such, important variables that impact wages such as age, years of education, type of education, years in the workforce, etc., are not controlled. When these factors are taken into account a completely different picture of today's workforce and the need for heavy-handed government intervention emerges.

Consider the following example. John Doe has a bachelor's degree and has worked continuously for the past ten years. His twin sister Jane has an associate's degree and has not worked three out of the last ten years due to the births of her two children. Given their different education levels and work history, it is only understandable that Jane's wages at the end of ten years would be lower.

Once other factors are taken into account, the wage gap is reduced considerably, sometimes becoming almost nonexistent. For example, women aged 27 to 33 without children earn 98 percent of what their male counterparts do.

The narrow wage gap between the men and women of Generation X reflects the tremendous gains that women have made over the last couple of generations. From 1989–2000, the number of women earning degrees increased by 26 percent. Nearly 1.7 million more women than men are currently enrolled in college. The wages of Ohio women, after adjusting for inflation, have increased by 10 percent over the last two decades.

Despite these tremendous gains made by women under a system of free enterprise, politicians continue to re-introduce comparable worth legislation. Comparable worth is a poor solution to a nonexistent problem. Replacing the market with politics is not in the best interests of Ohio's women or its economy.

"It is . . . imperative that employers do everything within their power to discourage, if not eliminate, all incidents of sexual harassment."

Workplace Sexual Harassment Laws Promote Justice for Women

Equal Rights Advocates

Equal Rights Advocates is an organization that works to protect and secure equal rights and economic opportunities for women through litigation and advocacy. In the following viewpoint the organization contends that a major problem keeping women from attaining equal rights and economic opportunities is sexual harassment in the workplace, which it contends is a widespread and serious problem. Women are unlikely to complain or resist being harassed or mistreated on the job, it argues, because of fears of losing their jobs. The author praises changes in federal civil rights law for strengthening legal remedies against sexual harassment, including making employers liable for damages when supervisors abuse their power over their subordinates.

As you read, consider the following questions:

1. Why do many cases of sexual harassment involve a worker and her direct supervisor, according to the Equal Rights Advocates?
2. What are the two kinds of sexual harassment, according to the author?
3. What are some of the costs to society of sexual harassment, according to Equal Rights Advocates?

S exual harassment is far more prevalent in the workplace than most people realize. A *Cornell Law Review* article entitled "Exacerbating the Exasperated: Title VII Liability of Employers for Sexual Harassment" reported that between 40% to 90% of women in the United States workforce have been the victims of some form of sexual harassment on the job. As even conservative Ninth Circuit Judge [Alex] Kozinski recognized: "It is a sobering revelation that every woman— *every* woman—who has spent time in the workforce in the last two decades can tell at least one story about being the object of sexual harassment."

The majority of incidents, particularly egregious incidents, occur between a supervisor and his subordinate. One study of Fortune 500 companies found that almost two thirds of sexual harassment complaints were brought against a woman's immediate supervisor or another person with greater power. Other studies have shown that half of all sexual harassers are the direct supervisors of their target, and that supervisors are more likely to engage in and get away with more severe forms of harassment.

The reason is plain: power is central to a supervisor's harassment of a subordinate. As a result, a victim of sexual harassment is more likely to submit to and less likely to complain when the harasser is a supervisor. Not only do supervisors have, by definition, greater authority and power than do their subordinates, but they also control the norms of the workplace. In addition to determining assignments, evaluating performance and recommending promotions, they influence the "climate" of work: what behaviors are acceptable, what standards exist and how communication occurs. Individuals in higher status positions believe and are believed to have the right to make demands of those in lower status roles. Some managers view harassing behavior as an extension of that right. They expect lower status individuals to comply.

Two Kinds of Sexual Harassment

There are two kinds of sexual harassment: "quid pro quo" and "hostile environment." *Quid pro quo*, a Latin term meaning "this for that," occurs when your boss offers you benefits, or threatens to change your working conditions, based on your response to his demands for sexual favors. "I'll give you a raise if you go out with me . . ." or "I'll demote you if you don't have sex with me" are examples of "quid pro quo" harassment. *Hostile environment* harassment occurs when physical, verbal, or visual sexual harassment is severe or pervasive enough to create a hostile or abusive work environment. This type of harassment does not require a loss or threat of loss of your job, or the promise of benefits. Comments about your body, sexual remarks, pornographic pictures displayed at the workplace, and touching and grabbing may all create a hostile work environment. In addition, the conduct must be unwelcome to you. If you like, want, or welcome the conduct, then you are not being sexually harassed. And if the conduct does not relate to your sex or have sexual references, it's not sexual harassment.

A single incident of inappropriate behavior is unlikely to be considered sexual harassment unless it's severe. For example, a single incident of rape or attempted rape would likely constitute sexual harassment (as well as violate criminal laws). However, a single unwanted request for a date or a single sexually suggestive comment, while offensive, may not be defined as sexual harassment. But a number of incidents that are relatively minor may amount to sexual harassment.

Because of the workplace hierarchy, the sexually harassed woman is unlikely to complain. Often, she is economically and emotionally dependent on her aggressor. Moreover, the abuse is humiliating, so the victim is motivated to keep it secret. Fearful of losing her job and economic security, she keeps quiet. She also may fear retraumatization by the legal system if she seeks recourse from higher authorities. Not surprisingly then, studies have shown repeatedly that very few individuals report their experiences or lodge an official complaint. Indeed, a review of ten studies revealed that only ten to fifteen percent of women either responded assertively to or reported the harassment. More than fifty percent of victims simply do and say nothing.

Changes in Civil Rights Law

Until 1991, Title VII entitled sexual harassment victims to collect only back pay, lost wages and, if they had been forced to leave, to be reinstated in their jobs. These women, if they won their cases, received a small monetary amount and an intolerable job back. Title VII of the Civil Rights Act of 1964, as amended in 1991, strengthened the remedies for sexual harassment. It allows sexual harassment victims to recover compensatory damages beyond back pay, and may do so in a jury trial. Moreover, these damages can encompass "future pecuniary losses, emotional pain, suffering, inconvenience, mental anguish, loss of enjoyment of life, and other nonpecuniary losses." Plaintiffs can also collect punitive damages, if they can demonstrate that an employer acted with malice or with reckless or callous indifference.

A Serious Problem in Schools

Sexual harassment is a common occurrence in school. In a survey by the American Association of University Women, more than one in 10 middle and high school girls reported being forced to perform a sexual act other than kissing; 65 percent said they had been grabbed or pinched; and 76 percent said they had faced unwanted sexual remarks, gestures or looks at school.

In case after case school officials are alleged to have known about harassment and done nothing. . . .

Every girl should be able to go to school without being groped or jeered. And parents should have the right to demand harassment-free schools for their children—even if they need a court order to do so.

National NOW Times, Spring 1999.

Against this backdrop, in 1998 the Supreme Court decided in *Ellerth v. Burlington Industries*, No. 97-569 and *Faragher v. City of Boca Raton*, No. 97-282 that companies may be held vicariously liable if supervisors sexually harass workers even if the employees do not report the harassment and suffered no tangible loss. By making employers liable for supervisors' sexual harassment encourages an employer, as no other regime does, to exercise the greatest possible care in screening prospective managers and in training, supervising and monitoring supervisory personnel. It gives employers an incentive to put effective policies and training programs in place. In fact, 54% of Fortune 500 employers admitted in one survey that fears of legal exposure prompted them to establish company policies against harassment. And experience has shown these policies and programs work. Companies that have implemented sexual harassment training programs have reported reduced numbers of claims that develop into lawsuits.

Society's Stake

Society has a great stake in ensuring that the alarming rate of sexual harassment goes down. A *Cleveland State Law Review* article entitled "The Present State of Sexual Harassment Law: Perpetuating Post Traumatic Stress Disorder in Sexually Harassed Women" reported that 90% to 95% of sexually harassed women suffer from some debilitating stress reaction, including anxiety, depression, headaches, sleep disorders, weight loss or gain, nausea, lowered self-esteem and sexual dysfunction. They experience job-related costs as well: from job loss, decreased morale, decreased job satisfaction to irreparable damage to interpersonal relationships at work. One study found that fully 50% of women who filed a complaint in California were fired; another 25% resigned due to the stresses of the complaint process or the harassment itself. A study of federal employees reported that those who have been harassed lose $4.4 million in wages and 973,000 hours in unpaid leave each year.

The costs are borne not only by the victims of harassment; they create financial havoc for employers as well. Sexual harassment costs a typical Fortune 500 company $6.7 million per year in absenteeism, low productivity and employee turnover. That does not include additional costs for litigation expenses, executive time and tarnished public image should a case wind up in court.

It is, therefore, imperative that employers do everything within their power to discourage, if not eliminate, all incidents of sexual harassment. Making them liable when supervisors abuse their power over subordinates is one small step in this direction. If they are made responsible, employers will have the incentive to create a workplace free of harassing behavior.

| "Sexual harassment regulation has failed
| women in a changing world."

Workplace Sexual Harassment Laws Do Not Promote Justice for Women

Joan Kennedy Taylor

Joan Kennedy Taylor maintains in the following viewpoint that sexual harassment laws aimed at protecting women at work are actually doing them harm. Such laws violate free speech and foster an antiquated view of women. The problems facing women in the workplace stem from a lack of understanding between men and women—not sexism, she contends. Women need to learn to protect themselves in workplace situations without government interference. Taylor is the author of *What to Do When You Don't Want to Call the Cops: A Non-adversarial Approach to Sexual Harassment.* She is also a founding member and past vice president of Feminists for Free Expression, an organization that works to defend First Amendment rights.

As you read, consider the following questions:

1. How has the American workforce changed, according to Taylor?
2. What comparison does the author make between sexual harassment law and earlier protective labor legislation?
3. What should women do about uncomfortable working situations, according to Taylor?

W e are letting something destructive happen to American business in the name of helping women. Current sexual harassment law—that is, the extension of anti-discrimination law to stifle and punish sexual speech in the workplace—is creating the very hostility between the sexes that it purports to correct.

Men and women are not natural enemies, but they are being told that they are. Men are warned that if they offend female co-workers they may be disciplined or even fired. Women are being instructed that offensive speech, if heard from men in the workplace, is probably illegal. And to top it off, the Supreme Court is requiring businesses to give those warnings.

Management Issues

There is certainly a free-speech issue involved, but from a management perspective the matter is worse than that: It's divisive. The workplace and society are changing. The American workforce is becoming more diverse and our work is less dependent on physical strength. Women are now needed in jobs for which, just a few decades ago, they had to struggle to be considered.

The problem is not one of sexism. It is one of expectation and communication, and of misinformation given to workers of both genders. There are undoubtedly a few men who bitterly resent the success of women. But their problem and problems of sexual predation and male aggression are not the subjects discussed in the ubiquitous programs management feels compelled to set up today. Rather, it's clear that those programs deal with faulty expectation and miscommunication: the joke couched in raw language, the seemingly playful insult, the complimentary remark, the hazing of a newcomer—in other words, the staples of male culture.

Women can't know the way men behave when women are not around. And men, used to all-male workplaces, are not always sure how to treat female co-workers. They may treat them as sex objects rather than colleagues or be overly paternalistic. But those faulty expectations and miscommunications do not prove sexual harassment.

If the problem is not one of sexism, the solution is not legal remedy. Instead, the solution is to increase all workers' knowledge and to facilitate communication. We need a different attitude and a different kind of employee training.

Wasserman. © by Tribune Media Services. Reproduced by permission.

This country tried once before to protect women from the effects of workplace transition. The protective labor legislation in effect from 1908 until the 1970s mandated special conditions for women: minimum wages, maximum hours, laws against night work and heavy lifting and requirements for special rest breaks. Certain occupations, like mining and wrestling, were closed to women altogether. Feminists realized in the 1970s that such regulations were "protecting" women out of good jobs and promotions.

Once more, an attempt to protect women at work is doing them harm. Like the earlier labor legislation, sexual harassment protection assumes that women are too delicate to flourish in the workplace without government aid.

Sexual harassment regulation has failed women in a changing world. It harms everyone. It violates free speech, creates rather than lessens workplace hostility and fosters a Victorian view of women. If some women find it difficult to speak up for themselves, we should endeavor to help them to empower themselves, not rely on the government regulation to mandate worker relations.

Women Cannot Rely on Government

Government not only should not be relied on in social situations, it cannot be relied on. Women can learn what to expect and how to handle it, and in so doing will not only better protect themselves but will also feel the satisfaction that comes from being effective personally as well as professionally.

Periodical Bibliography

The following articles have been selected to supplement the diverse views presented in this chapter.

Naomi Barko — "The Other Gender Gap," *American Prospect*, June 19, 2000.

Stephanie Boraas and William M. Rodgers III — "How Does Gender Play a Role in the Earnings Gap?" *Monthly Labor Review*, March 2003.

Michelle J. Budig — "Male Advantage and the Gender Composition of Jobs: Who Rides the Glass Escalator?" *Social Problems*, May 2002.

Philip N. Cohen and Matt L. Huffman — "Occupational Segregation and the Devaluation of Women's Work Across U.S. Labor Markets," *Social Forces*, March 2003.

Brian T. Farmer — "Politicizing the Pay Gap," *New American*, June 28, 2004.

Liza Featherstone — "Wal-Mart Values: Selling Women Short," *Nation*, December 16, 2002.

Margaret Gibelman — "So How Far Have We Come? Pestilent and Persistent Gender Gap in Pay," *Social Work*, January 2003.

Kimberly Goad — "When Guys Get Too Friendly: Groping Isn't Just Something That Happens in Hollywood," *Redbook*, February 2004.

E.J. Graff — "The M/F Boxes: Transgender Activists May Force Us to Rethink Basic Assumptions About Sex," *Nation*, December 17, 2001.

David Cay Johnston — "As Salary Grows, So Does a Gender Gap," *New York Times*, May 12, 2002.

G.L. Klienhardt — "It Happened to Me: I Never Thought I'd Experience Sexual Harassment," *Today's Christian Woman*, November/December 2001.

Julie N. Lynem — "A Decade Later, Hill's Impact Is Still Being Felt," *San Francisco Chronicle*, May 19, 2002.

Maclean's — "Women Still Face Workplace Barriers," June 26, 2000.

Karla Mantilla — "What Are We Working For? Equality or Radical Transformation?" *Off Our Backs*, January/February 2004.

Marc Spindelman — "Sex Equality Panic," *Columbia Journal of Gender and Law*, Winter 2004.

Jenny Strasburg

"Equality; Losing Ground; More than 40 Years After the Civil Rights Act, Why Do Women's Wages Still Trail Men's?" *San Francisco Chronicle*, January 9, 2005.

Gila Stopler

"Countenancing the Oppression of Women: How Liberals Tolerate Religious and Cultural Practices That Discriminate Against Women," *Columbia Journal of Gender and Law*, Winter 2003.

CHAPTER 4

Is Global Social Justice Being Upheld?

Chapter Preface

Economic inequality exists not only within the United States but between rich and poor nations of the world. The wealthy nations—which include the United States, Canada, Japan, and the nations of Western Europe—have a per capita gross domestic product twenty to more than one hundred times greater than impoverished nations such as Ethiopia, Afghanistan, and Bolivia. Within these poor nations, people struggle under conditions even worse than what the poor in the United States confront. A United Nations human development report assessing the 1990s provides some details about global poverty that Americans may find difficult to comprehend. "More than 13 million children have died through diarrhoeal disease in the past decade. Each year over half a million women, one for every minute of the day, die in pregnancy and childbirth. . . . For many countries the 1990s were a decade of despair. . . . In 34 [countries] life expectancy has fallen." The World Bank has estimated that 24 percent of the population in developing nations (about 1 billion people) live in absolute poverty, with incomes of less than one dollar a day.

This poverty, as well as the economic inequality found both within and between nations, raises several questions, including, what, if anything, do rich nations owe poor nations? Some argue that the people in developed nations have an ethical obligation to provide a certain amount of foreign aid to poor nations. They contend that the United States has not lived up to this obligation. The United Nations has established a target for wealthy nations: They should dedicate 0.7 percent of their gross national product to official development assistance. However, the United States gives less than .1 percent. Marian L. Tupy, an analyst with the libertarian Cato Institute, disagrees with those who believe that rich nations should give aid to poor nations. She contends that foreign aid fuels corruption among poor nations' leaders and retards economic policies that would benefit the people of developing nations. Foreign aid, Tupy contends, "expiates the guilt that we-the-rich feel for living a comfortable life, but does little to actually help the world's poor."

The appropriate level of foreign aid that rich nations should give to poor nations is but one of several controversies concerning the relationships among the world's countries. As trade and technology continue to make the world smaller and more interdependent, increasing numbers of people are confronting questions about how to promote economic and social justice on a global scale. The viewpoints in this chapter present several views on global social justice.

"Capitalist globalization provides a
challenge to the very possibility of
democracy [and] global justice."

The Global Capitalist System
Is Unjust

Kai Nielsen

The following viewpoint is excerpted from philosopher Kai
Nielsen's book *Globalization and Justice*. Nielsen argues that
while globalization need not be harmful if based on principles
of equality and meeting human needs, the global capitalist system found in today's world is a travesty of social justice. Global
capitalism has resulted in billions of people worldwide suffering from poverty, disease, and short life expectancy—problems
that he believes could be alleviated by a more equitable distribution of the world's wealth and resources. Nielsen further
criticizes what he views as the undermining of democracy in
many nations, where political and economic decisions are being removed from elected political leaders and placed in the
hands of international bodies such as the World Trade Organization (WTO) and the World Bank. Nielsen is professor emer-
itus of philosophy at the University of Calgary.

As you read, consider the following questions:

1. What distinction does Nielsen draw between
   globalization and capitalist globalization?
2. What statistics about the economic inequality among
   nations does the author cite?
3. What objections does Nielsen have to the Structural
   Adjustment Programs sponsored by the International
   Monetary Fund and the World Bank?

Why is globalization so bad? Or is it really so bad? In the first place . . . globalization per se is not bad. It is . . . *capitalist* globalization, with neoliberal globalization being the worst form of such globalization, that is bad. In a world with a different rationale—in a world committed to equality and liberty and to the maximal possible meeting of the human needs of everyone—globalization, of a certain sort, as an effective instrument for achieving that worldwide, would be a good thing; free trade, genuinely free trade, would be a good thing—there would, as there is not now, actually be the unimpeded circulation of goods to the benefit of everyone as well as the free circulation of peoples. We would become more internationalist and less ethnocentric and, with the free and extended circulation of peoples, our cultural life would be enriched. While most of us no doubt would continue to think of ourselves as members of groups which make us distinct peoples where typically we would cherish our distinctness, the very globalization process would make it easier, and with a more secure sense of reality, to *also* think of ourselves as a worldwide community of peoples and to cherish that thought.

So it is capitalism and not globalization which causes the trouble. Why say that? Well, for starters, 50,000 people die every day, a goodly number quite unnecessarily, where in many cases their deaths are easily preventable with even a little more equal world distribution of resources. But just the opposite is happening with capitalist globalization. The ratio of the richest countries in the world to the poorest has steadily increased under capitalism. In 1913 the ratio of the wealth of the richest countries in the world to that of the poorest was 11 to 1, in 1950 it was 35 to 1, in 1973 it was 44 to 1, in 1992 it was 72 to 1. The International Monetary Fund (IMF) and the World Bank, to take two key instruments of capitalist globalization, sponsored Structural Adjustment Programs[1] that have led to a doubling since 1971 of the number of countries in which per capita income is less than $900 per year. Approximately three billion people (a third of the world) live on less than $2 a day,

1. a set of policies and loan conditions that generally include privatizing public enterprises, reducing government debt and spending, increasing exports, and opening markets to foreign trade and investment

Why Inequality Matters

I think we should care about levels of inequality because as processes of globalization become stronger there is a much greater awareness of differences in income between different people and nations, and this influences people's attitudes and behavior. . . .

That creates lots of anger and negative feelings. Some people call it envy and treat it as somehow unacceptable. But even if this were the case, you cannot just rule envy out and forbid it to influence people's behavior. But treating it as envy is fundamentally wrong. One man's envy is another man's justice: a rich man considers each comparison of incomes to be a product of envy; a poor man might on the contrary see the same difference in incomes as unjust.

Branko Milanovic, *Multinational Monitor*, July/August 2003.

---

two billion are suffering from anemia, and as many people in the Third World have a very short life expectancy. A bad situation has been made worse by capitalist globalization. It creates poverty and inequality. Since 1950, the total dollar value of the world economy has increased fivefold while the number of people living in absolute poverty has doubled. Political leaders of capitalist countries . . . assume—or at least say they do—that globalization will ultimately bring convergence between the world's rich and poor. And some economists . . . back them up, though some do not. (One has the suspicion that economics, while thinking of itself as hardheaded and objective, is really rather politicized and often ideological.) *Perhaps* things will swing around that way, but the evidence now massively supports the claim that the rich are getting richer and the poor poorer and that there is nothing like even a trickle-down effect to improve the lot of the poorest. The level of absolute immiseration is actually growing. The amount of poverty, starvation, malnutrition, unemployment, lack of health care and drinkable water, the extent of infant mortality, and poverty-driven AIDS is rising. This is in considerable part due to the blessings of capitalist globalization.

The Democracy Deficit

While I have stressed the most tangible ill consequences of capitalist globalization, there are others as well. There is, to take one of the more obvious ones, the deficit in democracy caused by taking key political, economic, and cultural decisions out of the control of people and parliaments. That our elected leaders (presidents, prime ministers) voluntarily relinquish much such control to the WTO [World Trade Organization] and the like hardly makes it less undemocratic. We have gradually, over a long period of time, come to have what [German politician and philosopher] Ralf Dahrendorf calls a creeping authoritarianism, something which is accelerated by and exacerbated by capitalist globalization. The IMF, to take a key example, through Structural Adjustment Programs, now directly runs the economies of over seventy countries. That means that 1,000 capitalist economists control the economic policies for 1.4 billion people in those countries. *Maybe* such paternalism is justified, but it is certainly not democratic. Perhaps some neoliberals would bite that bullet, like libertarians they are not so keen on democracy, but social liberals such as T.H. Green, John Dewey, or John Rawls would not. Taking control over such a crucial aspect of the lives of over a billion people, taking control of an aspect which is so essential for their autonomy, would take, to put it minimally, a lot of justification indeed. People with any respect for human liberty at all cannot tolerate that. Regimes which support that cannot be, to be pleonastic, liberty-loving democracies. Their very democratic status is suspect.

These are not the only ills of capitalist globalization and much more needs to be said about such globalization, including a careful specification of what exactly it is. . . . But enough has been said already to show that capitalist globalization provides a challenge to the very possibility of democracy, global justice, and to the flourishing of humankind.

> "*The evidence is overwhelming that the past 30 years have witnessed a strong shift toward global equalization.*"

The Global Capitalist System Is Fair

Johan Norberg

Johan Norberg is a Swedish writer and researcher and the author of the book *In Defense of Global Capitalism*. In the following viewpoint he contends that globalization—which he defines as the process by which trade, investment, and other economic activities are increasingly crossing national borders—is a positive development that has improved the lives of most people. Globalization has especially helped residents of poor nations, who have seen their living standards and power over their own lives increased, he asserts. Norberg rebuts arguments that capitalist globalization creates economic inequality and exploits poor workers, arguing that politicians and others have made globalization a scapegoat for social problems.

As you read, consider the following questions:

1. How have the lives of people in India and China changed between the 1960s and 1990s, according to Norberg?
2. What two arguments does the author provide to refute the claim that a growing economic gap exists between wealthy and poor countries?
3. What defenses does Norberg make of "sweatshops" in the Third World?

U nder what is rather barrenly termed "globalization"— the process by which people, information, trade, investments, democracy, and the market economy tend more and more to cross national borders—our options and opportunities have multiplied. We don't have to shop at the big local company; we can turn to a foreign competitor. We don't have to work for the village's one and only employer; we can seek alternative opportunities. We don't have to make do with local cultural amenities; the world's culture is at our disposal. Companies, politicians, and associations have to exert themselves to elicit interest from people who have a whole world of options. Our ability to control our own lives is growing, and prosperity is growing with it.

Free markets and free trade and free choices transfer power to individuals at the expense of political institutions. . . .

To those of us in rich countries, more economic liberty to pick and choose may sound like a trivial luxury, even an annoyance—but it isn't. Fresh options are invaluable for all of us. And the existence from which globalization delivers people in the Third World—poverty, filth, ignorance, and powerlessness—really is intolerable. When global capitalism knocks at the door of Bhagant, an elderly agricultural worker and "untouchable" in the Indian village of Saijani, it leads to his house being built of brick instead of mud, to shoes on his feet, and clean clothes—not rags—on his back. Outside Bhagant's house, the streets now have drains, and the fragrance of tilled earth has replaced the stench of refuse. Thirty years ago Bhagant didn't know he was living in India. Today he watches world news on television. The stand that we in the privileged world take on the burning issue of globalization can determine whether or not more people will experience the development that has taken place in Bhagant's village. . . .

Globalization Improves Lives

People have a natural tendency to believe that everything is growing worse, and that things were better in the "old days." In 1014, Archbishop Wulfstan of York declared, "The world is in a rash and is getting close to its end."

Today, we hear that life is increasingly unfair amidst the market economy: "The rich are getting richer, and the poor are getting poorer." But if we look beyond the catchy slogans, we find that while many of the rich have indeed grown richer, so have most of the poor. Absolute poverty has diminished, and where it was greatest 20 years ago—in Asia—hundreds of millions of people have achieved a secure existence, even affluence, previously undreamed of. Global misery has diminished, and great injustices have started to unravel.

One of the most interesting books published in recent years is *On Asian Time: India, China, Japan 1966–1999*, a travelogue in which Swedish author Lasse Berg and photographer Stig Karlsson describe their visits to Asian countries during the 1960s. They saw poverty, abject misery, and imminent disaster. Like many, they could not bring themselves to hold out much hope for the future, and they thought that socialist revolution might be the only way out. Returning to India and China in the 1990s, they could not help seeing how wrong they were. More and more people have extricated themselves from poverty; the problem of hunger is steadily diminishing; the streets are cleaner. Squalid huts have given way to buildings wired for electricity with TV antennas on their roofs.

When Berg and Karlsson first visited Calcutta, fully one tenth of its inhabitants were homeless, and every morning trucks were sent by the public authorities or missionary societies to collect the bodies of those who had died in the night. Thirty years later, setting out to photograph people living on the streets, they had difficulty in *finding* such people. The rickshaw was disappearing from the urban scene, with people traveling by car, motorcycle, and subway instead.

When Berg and Karlsson showed young Indians photographs from the 1960s, they refused to believe it was even the same place. Could things really have been so dreadful? A striking illustration of the change is provided by a pair of photographs in their book. In the old picture, taken in 1976, a 12-year-old Indian girl named Satto holds up her hands. They are already furrowed and worn, prematurely aged by many years' hard work. The new picture shows Satto's 13-year-old daughter Seema, also holding up her hands. They are smooth and soft, the hands of a girl whose childhood has not been taken away from her.

137

The biggest change of all is in people's thoughts and dreams. Television and newspapers bring ideas and images from the other side of the globe, widening people's notions of the possible. Why make do with this kind of government when there are alternative political systems available?

Lasse Berg writes, self-critically:

Reading what we observers, foreigners as well as Indians, wrote in the '60s and '70s, nowhere in these analyses do I see anything of present-day India. Often nightmare scenarios—overpopulation, tumult, upheaval or stagnation—but not this calm and steady forward-jogging, and least of all this modernization of thoughts and dreams. Who foresaw that consumerism would penetrate so deeply in and among the villages? Who foresaw that both the economy and general standard of living would do so well? Looking back, what the descriptions have in common is an overstatement of the extraordinary, frightening uncertainty, and an understatement of the force of normality.

Note that all of the dramatic development described by Berg has resulted from sharp moves over the past few decades toward international capitalism and trade.

Globalization and Equality

This progress is all very well, many critics of globalization will argue, but even if the majority are better off, gaps have widened and wealthy people and countries have improved their lot more rapidly than others. The critics point out that 40 years ago the combined per capita GDP [gross domestic product] of the 20 richest countries was 15 times greater than that of the 20 poorest, and is now 30 times greater.

There are two reasons why this objection to globalization does not hold up. First, if everyone is better off, what does it matter that the improvement comes faster for some than for others? Only those who consider wealth a greater problem than poverty can find irritation in middle-class citizens becoming millionaires while the previously poverty-stricken become middle class.

Second, the allegation of increased inequality is simply wrong. The notion that global inequality has increased is largely based on figures from the U.N.'s 1999 *Human Development Report*. The problem with these figures is that they don't take into account what people can actually buy with their money. Without that "purchasing power" adjustment, the figures only show what a currency is worth on the international market, and nothing about local conditions. Poor people's actual living standards hinge on the cost of their food, their clothing, their housing—not what their money would get them while vacationing in Europe. That's why the U.N. uses purchasing-power-adjusted figures in other measures of living standards. It only resorts to the unadjusted figures, oddly, in order to present a theory of inequality.

A report from the Norwegian Institute for Foreign Affairs investigated global inequality by means of figures adjusted for purchasing power. Their data show that, contrary to conventional wisdom, inequality between countries has continuously *declined* ever since the end of the 1970s. This decline has been especially rapid since 1993, when globalization really gathered speed.

More recently, similar research by Columbia University development economist Xavier Sala-i-Martin has confirmed those findings. He found that when U.N. figures are adjusted for purchasing power, they point to a sharp decline in world inequality. Sala-i-Martin and co-author Surjit Bhalla also found independently that if we focus on inequality between *persons*, rather than inequality between *countries*, global inequality at the end of 2000 was at its lowest point since the end of World War II.

Estimates that compare countries rather than individuals, both authors note, grossly overestimate real inequality because they allow gains for huge numbers of people to be outweighed by losses for far fewer. For instance, country aggregates treat China and Grenada as data points of equal weight, even though China's population is 12,000 times Grenada's. Once we shift our focus to people rather than nations, the evidence is overwhelming that the past 30 years have witnessed a strong shift toward global equalization. . . .

Sweatshops

Advocates of protectionism often complain of "sweatshops" allegedly run by multinational corporations in the Third World. Let's look at the evidence: Economists have compared the conditions of people employed in American-owned facilities in developing countries with those of people employed elsewhere in the same country. In the poorest developing countries, the average employee of an American-affiliated company makes *eight times* the average national wage! In middle income countries, American employers pay *three times* the national average. Even compared with corresponding modern jobs in the same country, the multinationals pay about 30 percent higher wages. Marxists maintain that multinationals exploit poor workers. Are much higher wages "exploitation"?

The Standard of Living Is Rising Everywhere

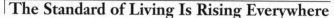

Living standards as measured by U.N. Human Development Index

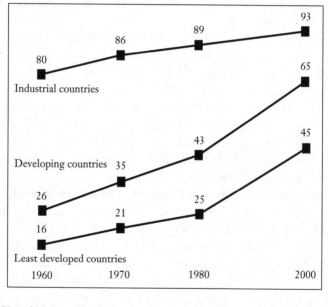

United Nations, *Human Development Report.*

The same marked difference can be seen in working conditions. The International Labor Organization has shown that multinationals, especially in the footwear and garment industries, are leading the trend toward better working conditions in the Third World. When multinational corporations accustom workers to better-lit, safer, and cleaner factories, they raise the general standard. Native firms then also have to offer better conditions, otherwise no one will work for them. Zhou Litai, one of China's foremost labor attorneys, has pointed out that Western consumers are the principal driving force behind the improvements of working conditions in China, and worries that "if Nike and Reebok go, this pressure evaporates."

One of the few Western participants in the globalization debate to have actually visited Nike's Asian subcontractors to find out about conditions there is Linda Lim of the University of Michigan. She found that in Vietnam, where the annual minimum wage was $134, Nike workers got $670. In Indonesia, where the minimum wage was $241, Nike's suppliers paid $720. If Nike were to withdraw on account of boycotts and tariffs imposed from the West, these employees would be put out of work and would move to more dangerous and less lucrative jobs in native industry or agriculture.

There are of course rogues among entrepreneurs, just as there are in politics, and all parts of life. But bad behavior by a few is no reason for banning large corporations from investing overseas. That would make no more sense than disbanding the police because we find instances of police brutality. . . .

A Scapegoat

Globalization makes an excellent scapegoat. It contains all the anonymous forces that have served this purpose throughout history: foreign countries, other races and ethnic groups, the uncaring market. Globalization does not speak up for itself when politicians blame it for overturning economies, increasing poverty, enriching a tiny minority, polluting the environment, or cutting jobs. And globalization doesn't usually get any credit when good things happen—an economy running at high speed, poverty diminishing, clearing skies. So if the trend toward greater global interchange and liberty is to continue, an ideological defense is needed.

In 25 years there are likely to be 2 billion more of us on this planet, and 97 percent of that population increase will occur in the developing world. There are no automatic processes deciding what sort of world they will experience. Most of that will depend on what people like you and me believe, think, and fight for.

Lasse Berg and Stig Karlsson record Chinese villagers' descriptions of the changes they experienced since the 1960s: "The last time you were here, people's thoughts and minds were closed, bound up," stated farmer Yang Zhengming. But as residents acquired power over their own livelihoods they began to think for themselves. Yang explains that "a farmer could then own himself. He did not need to submit. He decided himself what he was going to do, how and when. The proceeds of his work were his own. It was freedom that came to us. We were allowed to own things for ourselves."

Coercion and poverty still cover large areas of our globe. But thanks to globalizing economic freedom, people know that living in a state of oppression is not natural or necessary. People who have acquired a taste of economic liberty and expanded horizons will not consent to be shut in again by walls or fences. They will work to create a better existence for themselves. The aim of our politics should be to give them that freedom.

*"We are not against trade . . . but our
fear is that the global market intends
to annihilate our markets."*

Globalization Has Been Unfair
to the World's Poor

Jean-Bertrand Aristide

One of the most outspoken critics of globalization has been
Jean-Bertrand Aristide, who has twice been elected president
of Haiti. Aristide was first elected in 1990, deposed by a military coup in 1991, reinstalled as Haiti's president in 1994 with
the help of American troop support, elected to a second pres-
idential term in 2000, and forced out of office a second time
in 2004 amidst growing political unrest and pressure from
rebel groups and Haiti's military. While president, Aristide
was hailed by supporters as a strong advocate for the poor, but
detractors accused him of being repressive and corrupt. The
following viewpoint is excerpted from his 2000 book *Eyes of
the Heart: Seeking a Path for the Poor in the Age of Globalization.*
In it Aristide argues that global integration of the world's markets has caused much suffering among the world's poor and
has exacerbated a grossly unequal distribution of wealth. Haiti
and other nations that have opened their markets to world
trade have seen their economies destroyed and hunger and
poverty among their people increase, he argues.

As you read, consider the following questions:

1. What is the real crisis facing Haiti and other poor
   nations, according to Aristide?
2. What objections does the author make to foreign aid?

Our planet is entering the new century with fully 1.3 billion people living on less than one dollar a day. Three billion people, or half the population of the world, live on less than two dollars a day. Yet this same planet is experiencing unprecedented economic growth. The statistics that describe the accumulation of wealth in the world are mind-boggling. From where we sit, the most staggering statistics of all are those that reflect the polarization of this wealth. In 1960 the richest 20% of the world's population had 70% of the world's wealth, today they have 86% of the wealth. In 1960 the poorest 20% of the world's population had just 2.3% of the wealth of the world. Today this has shrunk to just barely 1%.

Imagine that the five fingers of your hand represent the world's population. The hand has $100 to share. Today the thumb, representing the richest 20% of the world's population, has $86 for itself. The little finger has just $1. The thumb is accumulating wealth with breathtaking speed and never looking back. The little finger is sinking deeper into economic misery. The distance between them grows larger every day.

A Human Crisis

Behind the crisis of dollars there is a human crisis: among the poor, immeasurable human suffering; among the others, the powerful, the policymakers, a poverty of spirit which has made a religion of the market and its invisible hand. A crisis of imagination so profound that the only measure of value is profit, the only measure of human progress is economic growth.

We have not reached the consensus that to eat is a basic human right. This is an ethical crisis. This is a crisis of faith.

Global capitalism becomes a machine devouring our planet. The little finger, the men and women of the poorest 20%, are reduced to cogs in this machine, the bottom rung in global production, valued only as cheap labor, otherwise altogether disposable. The machine cannot and does not measure their suffering. The machine also does not measure the suffering of our planet. Every second an area the size of a soccer field is deforested. This fact alone should be mobilizing men and women to protect their most basic interest—oxygen. But the machine overwhelms us. The distance between the thumb and the little finger stretches to the breaking point.

A Choice Between Death and Death

A morgue worker is preparing to dispose of a dozen corpses. One living soul lifts himself off the table, shakes his head and declares, "I am not dead!" To which the morgue worker answers, "Yes you are. The doctors say that you are dead, so lie down."

In today's global marketplace trillions of dollars are traded each day via a vast network of computers. In this market no one talks, no one touches. Only numbers count.

And yet today this faceless economy is already five times larger than the real, or productive, economy.

We know other marketplaces. On a plain high in the mountains of Haiti, one day a week thousands of people still gather. This is the marketplace of my childhood in the mountains above Port Salut. The sights and the smells and the noise and the color overwhelm you. Everyone comes. If you don't come you will miss everything. The donkeys tied and waiting in the woods number in the thousands. Goods are displayed in every direction: onions, leeks, corn, beans, yams, cabbage, cassava, and avocados, mangoes and every tropical fruit, chickens, pigs, goats, and batteries, and tennis shoes, too. People trade goods and news. This is the center; social, political, and economic life roll together. A woman teases and coaxes her client: "*Cherie*, the onions are sweet and waiting just for you." The client laughs and teases back until they make a deal. They share trade, and laughter, gossip, politics, and medical and child-rearing tips. A market exchange, and a human exchange.

We are not against trade, we are not against free trade, but our fear is that the global market intends to annihilate our markets. We will be pushed to the cities, to eat food grown on factory farms in distant countries, food whose price depends on the daily numbers game of the first market. "This is more efficient," the economists say. "Your market, your way of life, is not efficient," they say. But we ask, "What is left when you reduce trade to numbers, when you erase all that is human?"

Globalization, the integration of world markets, has promised to "lift all boats," rich and poor, to bring a global culture of entertainment and consumer goods to everyone— the promise of material happiness. And indeed, since 1980 most Third World countries have embraced globalization.

They have opened their economies to the world, lowered tariffs, embraced free trade, and allowed goods and services from the industrialized world to flow in. It seems the world is brought closer together. In fact the gap between the thumb and the little finger has never been larger.

AN EXPANDING FREE MARKET EXTENDS ALL BELLIES

Kirk. © 1998 by Kirk Anderson. Reproduced by permission.

What happens to poor countries when they embrace free trade? In Haiti in 1986 we imported just 7,000 tons of rice, the main staple food of the country. The vast majority was grown in Haiti. In the late 1980s Haiti complied with free trade policies advocated by the international lending agencies and lifted tariffs on rice imports. Cheaper rice immediately flooded in from the United States, where the rice industry is subsidized. In fact the liberalization of Haiti's market coincided with the 1985 Farm Bill in the United States which increased subsidies to the rice industry, so that 40% of U.S. rice growers' profits came from the government by 1987. Haiti's peasant farmers could not possibly compete. By 1996 Haiti was importing 196,000 tons of foreign rice at the cost of $100 million a year. Haitian rice production became negligible. Once the dependence on foreign rice was complete, import prices began to rise, leaving Haiti's population, particularly the urban poor, completely at the whim of rising world grain prices. And the prices continue to rise.

What lessons do we learn? For poor countries free trade is not so free, or so fair. Haiti, under intense pressure from the international lending institutions stopped protecting its domestic agriculture while subsidies to the U.S. rice industry increased. A hungry nation became hungrier. . . .

Foreign Aid

Many in the First World imagine the amount of money spent on aid to developing countries is massive. In fact, it amounts to only .03% of GNP [gross national product] of the industrialized nations. In 1995, the director of the U.S. aid agency defended his agency by testifying to his congress that 84¢ of every dollar of aid goes back into the U.S. economy in goods and services purchased. For every dollar the United States puts into the World Bank, an estimated $2 actually goes into the U.S. economy in goods and services. Meanwhile in 1995, severely indebted low-income countries paid $1 billion more in debt and interest to the International Monetary Fund (IMF) than they received from it. For the 46 countries of Sub-Saharan Africa, foreign debt service was four times their combined governmental health and education budgets in 1996. So, we find that aid does not aid.

The little finger knows that she is sinking deeper into misery each day, but all the while the thumb is telling her that profits are increasing, economies are growing and he is pouring millions of dollars of aid into her country. Whose profit? Whose economy? What aid? The logic of global capitalism is not logical for her. We call this economic schizophrenia.

Haiti's Pigs

The history of the eradication of the Haitian Creole pig population in the 1980s is a classic parable of globalization. Haiti's small, black, Creole pigs were at the heart of the peasant economy. An extremely hearty breed, well adapted to Haiti's climate and conditions, they ate readily available waste products, and could survive for three days without food. Eighty to 85% of rural households raised pigs; they played a key role in maintaining the fertility of the soil and constituted the primary savings bank of the peasant population. Traditionally a pig was sold to pay for emergencies and special occasions (funerals, marriages, baptisms, illnesses and, critically, to pay school fees and buy books for the children when school opened each year in October).

In 1982 international agencies assured Haiti's peasants their pigs were sick and had to be killed (so that the illness would not spread to countries to the North). Promises were made that better pigs would replace the sick pigs. With an efficiency not since seen among development projects, all of the Creole pigs were killed over a period of 13 months.

Two years later the new, better pigs came from Iowa. They were so much better that they required clean drinking water (unavailable to 80% of the Haitian population), imported feed (costing $90 a year when the per capita income was about $130), and special roofed pigpens. Haitian peasants quickly dubbed them as *"prince à quatre pieds,"* (four footed princes). Adding insult to injury, the meat did not taste as good. Needless to say, the repopulation program was a complete failure. One observer of the process estimated that in monetary terms, Haitian peasants lost $600 million. There was a 30% drop in enrollment in rural schools, there was a dramatic decline in the protein consumption in rural Haiti, a devastating decapitalization of the peasant economy, and an incalculable negative impact on Haiti's soil and agricultural productivity. The Haitian peasantry has not recovered to this day.

Most of rural Haiti is still isolated from global markets, so for many peasants the extermination of the Creole pigs was their first experience of globalization. The experience looms large in the collective memory. Today, when the peasants are told that "economic reform" and privatization will benefit them they are understandably wary. The state-owned enterprises are sick, we are told, and they must be privatized. The peasants shake their heads and remember the Creole pigs.

The 1997 sale of the state-owned flour mill confirmed their skepticism. The mill sold for a mere $9 million, while estimates place potential yearly profits at $20-30 million a year. The mill was bought by a group of investors linked to one of Haiti's largest banks. One outcome seems certain: This sale will further concentrate wealth—in a country where 1% of the population already holds 45% of the wealth of the country.

Choices of Globalization

If we have lingering doubts about where poor countries fall in this "new" economic order, listen to the World Bank. In September 1996, *The London Guardian* newspaper cited a draft World Bank strategy paper that predicted that the majority of Haitian peasants—who make up 70% of Haiti's population—are unlikely to survive bank-advocated free market measures. The Bank concluded: "The small volume of production and the environmental resource constraints will leave the rural population with only two possibilities: to work in the industrial or service sector, or to emigrate." At present the industrial sector employs only about 20,000 Haitians. There are already approximately 2.5 million people living in Port-au-Prince, 70% of them are officially unemployed and living in perhaps the most desperate conditions in the Western Hemisphere. Given the tragic history of Haiti's boat people, emigration, the second possibility, can hardly be considered a real option.

The choices that globalization offers the poor remind me of a story. Anatole, one of the boys who had lived with us at Lafanmi Selavi,[1] was working at the national port. One day a very powerful businessman offered him money to sabotage the main unloading forklift at the port. Anatole said to the man, "Well, then I am already dead." The man, surprised by the response, asked, "Why?" Anatole answered: "Because if I sneak in here at night and do what you ask they will shoot me, and if I don't, you will kill me." The dilemma is, I believe, the classic dilemma of the poor: a choice between death and death. Either we enter a global economic system, in which we know we cannot survive, or we refuse, and face death by slow starvation. With choices like these the urgency of finding a third way is clear. We must find some room to maneuver, some open space simply to survive. We must lift ourselves up off the morgue table and tell the experts we are not yet dead.

1. Lafanmi Selavi is the center for street children in Port-au-Prince founded by Aristide in 1986.

"*Overall, the process of globalization has
been good for the poor.*"

Globalization Has Been Fair to
the World's Poor

Doug Bandow

Critics of globalization often assert that people in poorer nations are becoming worse off. In the viewpoint that follows,
Doug Bandow argues that those who oppose globalization
fail to realize that integrating the world's poor within the
global economy is the best way to improve their lives and lift
them out of poverty. Activists who seek to stop globalization
would essentially condemn poor people in developing nations to lives of poverty and stagnation—a stance Bandow
condemns as immoral. Bandow is a senior fellow at the Cato
Institute, a libertarian think tank, and the author of several
books, including *Wealth, Poverty, and Human Destiny*.

As you read, consider the following questions:
1. Why is the process of developing a modern economy
   often painful, according to Bandow?
2. How does the author respond to the argument that
   Third World factory workers make low wages?
3. What are the political ramifications of globalization,
   according to Bandow?

D espite the worst efforts of violent protestors in Quebec, leaders of countries throughout the Western hemisphere concluded their Summit of the Americas by proposing a broad free-trade agreement.[1] Bringing more of the world's poor into the global economy is the best hope for raising them out of poverty.

Curiously, globalization has become the latest cause celebre of left-wing activists. These First-World demonstrators self-righteously pose as defenders of Third-World peoples, even as they advocate leaving the latter destitute.

Development Cannot Be Shut Off

The process of development, of moving traditional, agricultural societies into the Industrial and Information age, is extraordinarily painful. It was difficult enough for Western societies, which took hundreds of years to develop. It is even harder for today's developing states, which are attempting to telescope the process into a few decades.

But that pain must be endured to achieve a better life. Economist Joseph Schumpeter termed capitalism "creative destruction." Every innovation creates losers: automobiles ruined the buggy industry, computers destroyed the typewriter industry.

It is fair to encourage the development of social institutions to ease the transition. It is not fair to shut off development.

Rural Poverty

Some trendy Western activists wax eloquent on the wonders of rural living. Presumably they have never visited a poor country, let alone a poor countryside.

For instance, when I traveled the hills of eastern Burma with the relief group Christian Freedom International, I found ethnic Karen villagers living in wooden huts open to rain and insects. There was neither electricity nor running water. People lacked latrines and let their livestock run loose; filth was everywhere.

In such circumstances, life is hard, disease is rampant, and

---

1. Anti-globalization protesters who oppose free trade clashed with police during the April 2001 summit.

151

hope is nonexistent. No wonder people flee to the city. Not one Quebec protestor would likely choose such a "dignified" way of life.

Indeed, the problems of globalization must always be "compared to what?" Yes, factories pay low wages in Third World countries. But workers in them have neither the education nor the skills to be paid at First World levels.

Their alternative is not a Western university education or Silicon Valley computer job, but an even lower-paying job with a local firm or unemployment. The choice is clear: according to Edward Graham of the Institute of International Economics, in poor countries, American multinationals pay foreign citizens an average of 8.5 times the per capita GDP [gross domestic product].

Overall, the process of globalization has been good for the poor. During the 1980s, advanced industrialized countries grew faster than developing states. In the 1990s, as globalization accelerated, poor nations grew at 3.6 percent annually, twice that of their richer neighbors.

The Need for Economic Liberty

Despite the illusion of left-wing activists that money falls from the sky, poverty has been the normal condition of humankind throughout most of history. As even [Karl] Marx acknowledged, capitalism is what eliminated the overwhelming poverty of the pre-industrial world.

That remains the case today. Resource endowment, population level and density, foreign aid transfers, past colonial status, none of these correlate with economic wealth. Only economic openness does.

The latest [2001] volume of the *Economic Freedom in the World Report*, published by the Cato Institute and think tanks in 50 other countries, finds that economic liberty strongly correlates with economic achievement. Policies that open economies strongly correlate with economic growth.

By pulling countries into the international marketplace, globalization encourages market reforms. With them comes increased wealth.

Concern over the distribution of income understandably remains, but if nothing is produced, there is nothing to dis-

Multinational Corporations Help the Poor

There is a fierce debate today between those who consider globalization to be a malign influence on poor nations and those who find it a positive force. This debate focuses not just on trade, but also on multinational corporations. The hard evidence strongly suggests that the positive view is more realistic. There are many reasons to believe that multinationals in particular do good, not harm, in the developing world. . . .

Let's look at the facts on wage payments. Good empirical studies have been conducted in Bangladesh, Mexico, Shanghai, Indonesia, Vietnam, and elsewhere. And these studies find that multinationals actually pay what economists call a "wage premium," that is, an average wage that *exceeds* the going rate in the area where they are located. Affiliates of some U.S. multinationals pay a premium over local wages that ranges from 40 to 100 percent.

Jagdish Bhagwati, *American Enterprise*, June 2004.

tribute. And, in fact, globalization has shared its benefits widely. In a recent World Bank report, economists David Dollar and Aart Kraay conclude that the "income of the poor rises one-for-one with overall growth."

Political Ramifications

Globalization also has important political ramifications. Freedom is indivisible; economic liberty tends to undercut political controls. Countries such as South Korea and Taiwan threw off authoritarian dictatorships once their burgeoning middle classes demanded political rights to match economic opportunities.

International investment and trade also help dampen nationalism and militarism. Globalization is not enough: rising levels of foreign commerce did not prevent World War I, for instance.

Yet investment and trade create important economic incentives for peace. They also put a human face on people who might otherwise seem to be the enemy. The result is a better environment in which to promote international harmony.

Like most human phenomena, globalization has ill, as well as good, effects. But the latter predominate. In most ways for most people, globalization is a positive.

By seeking to destroy this process, the Quebec demonstrators would keep the world's poor outside of the global economy. The more responsible strategy is to build moral restraints and social institutions to ensure that those with the fewest options are not left behind as the forces of globalization transform their lives and societies.

| "The wealth of the world's 497 richest people is now greater than the combined incomes of the poorest half of the planet."

Capitalism Must Be Overthrown

Ken Boettcher

Ken Boettcher argues in the following viewpoint that the division of the world's people into a wealthy elite and the impoverished rest demonstrates the fundamental injustice of capitalism. Citing a study finding that the combined wealth of the billionaires in the world was greater than the combined annual incomes of the poorest half of the world's population, he argues that the world's wealth should not be under the control of a tiny minority. The solution, Boettcher concludes, is a socialist revolution in which the world's wealth is shared by all and used to combat such problems as hunger and poverty. Boettcher is an activist with the Socialist Labor Party and is on the staff of its newspaper, the *People*.

As you read, consider the following questions:

1. What argument does Boettcher make about the mass media?
2. What objections does the author raise about reforms and organized labor?
3. What would a democratic socialist system look like, according to Boettcher?

L ittle so blatantly demonstrates the continued absurdity of the division of the world's population into ruling and ruled classes—and accordingly the imperative need to build a world *without* classes if abundance, peace and the pursuit of happiness are to be had by all—than the yearly figures on the number of billionaires released by that unapologetic defender of capitalist-class rule, *Forbes* magazine.

What? *Forbes* demonstrating the obscenity of class rule in today's world? Well, not by itself. It is in juxtaposition with other figures that the 16-year-old *Forbes'* list of billionaires takes on its real significance. This spring [2002] that service was provided by the Institute for Policy Studies. IPS, in its own words, says that each year it "studies the list of the world's billionaires and tries to put their wealth in perspective by comparing it to other things that are big and important in the world."

Among the comparisons IPS drew from *Forbes'* list for 2001, which reported a total of 497 billionaires worldwide, was this astounding fact: the "collective wealth of the 497 is . . . greater than the combined incomes of the poorest half of humanity."

An Obscene Reality

Pause for just a moment here and let that comparison sink in. The wealth of the world's 497 richest people is now greater than the *combined* incomes of the poorest half of the *planet*.

On the very face of it one would think this obscene reality would spur millions to action across the face of the planet to change the way humanity worldwide organizes, produces and distributes goods and services—the economic wealth produced *collectively* by great masses of workers and peasants, in great industries built by workers where thousands come together to produce the world's wealth.

Why is it that today the world still accepts such an absurdity when it seems so apparent that a tiny minority is *privately* appropriating the vast majority of humanity's collectively produced wealth, and that the majority is therefore virtually enslaved to this tiny class of owners?

It is so for the very same reason that such a tiny minority at the very top of the capitalist heap—and an only marginally larger minority that owns and controls the vast majority of wealth produced by *all* the world's working classes—is able to appropriate this wealth. By virtue of its ownership and control of the means of life, this tiny minority controls far more than the economic sphere of human life.

As Karl Marx put it in the preface to *A Contribution to the Critique of Political Economy*, "In the social production of their existence, men inevitably enter into definite relations, which are independent of their will, namely relations of production appropriate to a given stage in the development of their material forces of production. The totality of these relations of production constitutes the economic structure of society, the real foundation, on which arises a legal and political super-structure and to which correspond definite forms of social consciousness. The mode of production conditions the general process of social, political and intellectual life."

Control of the Media

Virtually every source of mass information, especially of mass-distributed print and broadcast news and information—but also including films, the pulpit and the educational system—provides a conduit for promoting continued capitalist-class rule. Privately owned by and operated in the profit interests of capitalists, and supported primarily by the paid advertising of other capitalists, the major media have a material interest in propagandizing workers to accept capitalism and to ignore their own distinct interests as members of the working class. Likewise dependent upon the economic resources of the capitalist class are the educational system and organized religion.

Even the reform-minded among these elements do workers a disservice. Today's growing social, economic and environmental crises cry out for a *fundamental* transformation of society, while reformers seek to prune the most ugly fruit of a system whose whole trunk has long since gone to rot.

So-called "organized labor" also cannot be trusted to counter this influence. Based on the false principle that the interests of the capitalist class and the working class can be reconciled, these unions and their papers are the voices of the labor *faker*. They speak for the interests of those who *pose* as

Martin Luther King Jr. on Compassion and Justice

True compassion is more than flinging a coin to a beggar; it is not haphazard and superficial. It comes to see that an edifice which produces beggars needs re-structuring. A true revolution of values will soon look uneasily on the glaring contrast of poverty and wealth.

With righteous indignation, it will look across the seas and see individual capitalists of the West investing huge sums of money in Asia, Africa, and South America, only to take the profits out with no concern for the social betterment of the countries, and say: "This is not just."

Martin Luther King Jr., speech before Clergy and Laity Concerned, April 4, 1967.

---

representatives of labor but have a material stake in the business of packaging groups of workers and selling them out, in the process of selling "labor peace" to their exploiters.

Hope for Change

These facts do not mean that there is no hope for the world to change. As Marx continued in the preface to his *Critique of Political Economy*, "At a certain stage of development, the material forces of society come into conflict with the existing relations of production or—this merely expresses the same thing in legal terms—with the property relations within the framework of which they have operated hitherto. From forms of development of the productive forces these relations turn into their fetters. Then begins an era of social revolution. The changes in the economic foundation lead sooner or later to the transformation of the whole immense superstructure."

In the end, historic forces, including capitalism's cyclical and ever worsening economic crises and continually intensified class antagonisms, will arouse today's ruled classes to a consciousness of the evil of class rule and private ownership of the means of life, and they will resist and overcome capitalist rule. In the end, workers will become aware that capitalism long ago outlived its usefulness in the historic development of the world's productive forces, and that today it merely acts as a fetter upon the further development of human society. Meanwhile, all Socialists must denounce the wage system, under which the mass of useful producers are virtually the slaves of the tiny minority who perform no socially useful labor whatever, but merely own.

Join the Fight

All forward-thinking people must openly take the side of the working class in this struggle. Starting from the proposition that labor alone is the source of all social wealth, they must follow where fact and social science lead, to the only logical resolution of the class struggle: the abolition of capitalism and the creation of a socialist society, owned and controlled by the producers themselves.

Only under such a truly democratic, socialist system will the vast means of social wealth production in existence today—but which today is controlled by so incredibly few—become available to alleviate and eventually end the massive problems of hunger, poverty, war, racism and environmental crises that face humanity today.

"*In view of the bloody . . . history of the twentieth century, we have no excuse for thinking that the world could be made more just by abandoning capitalism.*"

There Are No Just Alternatives to Capitalism

John Isbister

John Isbister is a professor of economics at the University of California at Santa Cruz and the author of several books, including *Capitalism and Justice*, from which the following viewpoint is excerpted. Isbister begins by conceding that capitalism lacks many attributes of social justice, including equal treatment and freedom. However, Isbister goes on to argue that alternatives to capitalism, such as socialism and communism, have been tried and have been found even more wanting in social justice than capitalism. There is no choice but to work within the capitalist system to achieve social justice, Isbister concludes.

As you read, consider the following questions:

1. How does Isbister describe the world before the advent of capitalism in the sixteenth century?
2. Why does the author characterize communism as a "dream"?
3. In what ways have Communist societies failed, according to to Isbister?

John Isbister, *Capitalism and Justice: Envisioning Social and Economic Fairness*. Bloomfield, CT: Kumarian Press, 2001. Copyright © 2001 by Kumarian Press, Inc. All rights reserved. Reproduced by permission.

Capitalism left to its own devices fails to produce social justice. It does not give us equality, freedom, or efficiency. It produces inequalities of both opportunities and outcomes. It expands the freedom of some people at the expense of others. It produces economic growth, but erratically. . . .

Many who have arrived at roughly this position have concluded, reasonably enough, that if capitalism can guarantee neither freedom nor equal treatment, it should be replaced. This is no longer a viable position, however. There is no point seeking alternatives to capitalism, for two separate reasons.

The first reason is that noncapitalist systems have been tried and for the most part have been found to be even less just than capitalism. In view of the bloody and tumultuous history of the twentieth century, we have no excuse for thinking that the world could be made more just by abandoning capitalism.

The second reason is that capitalism is all we have. Precapitalist social formations—tribes, isolated villages, feudal arrangements, and the rest—are almost gone, destroyed by capitalist imperialism, trade, investment, and technology. Socialism and communism were once thought to be the natural successors of capitalism, but as forms of social and economic organization they too have almost disappeared. Capitalist relationships characterize most local communities, almost all states, and certainly the international relationships between states. The next two sections advance this argument in more detail.

Precapitalism: The Organic Community

Capitalism arose in Europe in the sixteenth century and spread by means of commerce and imperialism (often the two were indistinguishable) to the rest of the world. Everywhere it expanded it destroyed what had come before: manorial, feudal systems of different sorts in Europe and a variety of tribal, communal, and imperial systems in the rest of the world. The old systems did not disappear easily; their going was attended by conflict and bloodshed. . . .

In most parts of the precapitalist world, at most times, people were members of an integrated, organic community in which they had both rights and responsibilities, guaranteed by the fact of being born. These were typically spiritual as well as secular communities, in which the gods were thought to be present and active in all aspects of life. In many precapitalist communities, people's principal tasks were to emulate their ancestors and to please the spirits.

Was it a just world, just in a sense that might have meaning for us today? Can we turn to the precapitalist world to give us a vision of how to live our lives? For the most part, no. Few precapitalist societies had ideas of justice that are congenial to us today. The caste or class system was generally rigid; one's fate in life was largely determined by the accident of birth. People enjoyed virtually none of the freedoms associated with, say, the Bill of Rights. Rulers ruled and subjects obeyed. Wars were endemic and punishments often cruel. The European feudal world was an organic community in which people belonged and were not abandoned, but it was a world of exploitation and harshness for most of its members. Few of us would want to live in the Aztec culture, to take another example, or in most of the precapitalist societies of which we have some knowledge. . . .

Some in the capitalist world try to retain or re-create the best parts of precapitalism. Some Amish and Mennonite communities are based on precapitalist values, as are some other faith-based groups. The 1960s and 1970s saw the creation of secular alternative rural communes, communities whose members tried to eliminate all marks of distinction between them, to be self-sufficient, and to live simply. The communes had some successes, but most eventually collapsed. Communities such as these have attempted to embody precapitalist values, but none has succeeded in cutting itself off from capitalist influences: from the market, from the media, from the legal system, and from other influences of the modern world. While we can learn from our antecedent societies, we cannot return to them. That door has been closed.

Postcapitalism: The Transcendent Dream

The most serious challenges to capitalism have come not from those who wanted to return to a simpler world but from people with an alternate—socialist or communist—vision of an economically advanced society. [Karl] Marx and the early socialist thinkers accepted what they understood as the virtue of capitalism—that it had produced unprecedented economic growth and thereby had created the potential for a high standard of living for everyone. Capitalism had, however, brought with it exploitation, alienation, and injustice, all of which they believed could be overcome in the new socialist world that would replace capitalism. For a later generation, communism was not the successor to capitalism but its substitute, a more humane and efficient system for transforming nonindustrial societies like Russia and China.

As [Harvard historian] Michael Ignatieff argues, many communists understood their movement as embodying the science of history, but communism was really the opposite; it was a dream. It was a dream held by nineteenth- and twentieth-century people who were intensely aware of the injustices of the capitalist system in which they lived. They were revolted by the crassness of capitalism, by the huge gap between the rich and the poor, by the way in which the system used up and discarded millions of people, by the replacement of human values with the values of money and accumulation, and by the warfare that they understood as a direct consequence of capitalist competition. Against the inhuman face of capitalism, they posited the image of "the new man," the socialist man (not until its later years was socialism at all infused with feminism), the man whose values were focused on a concern for his community and for his fellows, not distorted and narrowed by competition and accumulation. In the socialist dream, the community's resources and assets were to be owned collectively by the people and used to fulfill the people's real needs. The new economic principle was to be, in the words of Marx and [Friedrich] Engels, "from each according to his abilities, to each according to his needs." The state was a pure democracy, or in some versions there was no state at all. With the end of capitalism would come the end of nationalism, and with the end of nationalism the end of war.

It was an extraordinary dream, a dream so powerful that for many people it persisted long after the evidence showed that it was failing. In the middle years of the twentieth century, some communists abandoned the dream as the government of the Soviet Union committed one atrocity after another—but others stayed faithful, presumably because the dream had such meaning for them and also because the alternative, the continuation of the advanced capitalist system, seemed so ghastly.

Nevertheless, the dream failed. In many ways, the communist regimes of the twentieth century brought the opposite of justice. [Vladimir] Lenin and [Joseph] Stalin in the Soviet Union, Mao Zedong in China, Kim Il Sung in North Korea, Pol Pot in Cambodia, and many of their subordinates and imitators were responsible for far more deaths among their innocent countrymen than even [Adolf] Hitler. While the Nazis can be held accountable for about 25 million deaths, the latest scholarship attributes between 85 and 100 million deaths to eighty years of communist rule. Millions were consigned to labor camps without the niceties of a fair trial. Democracy was abandoned, as a vestige of corrupt and bourgeois capitalism.

Capitalism and Freedom

Capitalism is freedom—and freedom leads to prosperity. The moral is the practical. On the other hand, statism is oppression—and oppression leads to destitution. The immoral is the impractical. After two centuries of capitalism, 80 years of socialism, and a millennium of feudalism, the contest is over and the scores are on the board. The alternatives open to human beings are stark: freedom and prosperity or statism and misery. We have only to make our choice.

Andrew Bernstein, *Freeman*, December 2003.

Many of the communist regimes produced remarkable economic growth, but in the end even this could not save them from collapse. The major communist revolutions occurred in precapitalist societies. The economic function of the Soviet state, to take the leading communist example, was to create a modern industrial system. In just two generations, despite the terrible burdens of two world wars, it succeeded in turning a backward, rural society into an urbanized, industrial society with a relatively healthy, literate, and productive population, with substantial social services and with world-class scientific and cultural establishments. But it was not enough. The human costs were monstrous, and in the end the Soviet economic system could produce neither the food nor the consumer goods demanded by an urbanized population. Marxist orthodoxy was that capitalism was the engine of economic growth and that once capitalism had done its work of raising productive capacity it would be replaced by a socialist system concerned with the needs not of the capitalists but of the people. The actual history of twentieth-century Russia looks much the opposite: communism was the engine of industrial growth, but it could not meet people's needs for consumer goods, for freedom, and for human rights, so once it had done its work of economic growth it was replaced by a version of capitalism. Whether Russian capitalism will be more respectful of the people's needs is yet to be seen. . . .

Democratic Socialists and Social Democrats

Some who remained true to the dream in the face of the actual performance of many of the communist regimes argued that those regimes did not represent true communism, that Stalin, Mao, and the others had betrayed communist and socialist principles. The "democratic socialists" in the West, a group of people on the whole honorable, visionary, and compassionate, held that if it was to be responsible to the real needs of the people, socialism had to answer to the people. This principle informed most of the Western socialist parties, including the British Labor Party and the New Democratic Party and its antecedents in Canada. They accepted the constraints of democratic, electoral systems. To gain power in a genuinely democratic system, however, the democratic socialists had to give up most of their socialist principles, including state ownership of the means of production. The Labor government in Britain after the Second World War brought about some real transformations, including the nationalization of a number of the country's most important industries. In subsequent years, however, Conservative governments reversed the nationalizations, and Labor found that it could return to power only if it explicitly rejected its former principles. The story is common to most Western capitalist countries; the socialist parties converted themselves into somewhat left-of-center capitalist parties, arguing for a more generous welfare program, but nothing more radical. One way of understanding the change is to say that the democratic socialists became social democrats. None of the Western socialist parties currently challenges the system of private enterprise. Some academics still make proposals for what they hope might be a humane version of socialism, but these ideas garner little public support.

The communist societies have almost completely disappeared. Not the communist political parties or in some cases the communist totalitarian states—plenty of them still exist, in Vietnam, China, and many other countries. With a few exceptions, however, the communist system of economic and social organization has gone. In Russia, state control of the economy was replaced by a kind of anarchic and unpredictable banditry. The former satellite states of eastern Europe moved in varying degrees toward capitalist markets. The Chinese Communist Party relaxed its control of the economy, encouraging private ownership, entrepreneurship, and foreign investment. In Vietnam, as in China, the party maintained control over the political system, but the economy was increasingly based on capitalist principles. At the beginning of the twenty-first century, only two national societies are still organized on communist principles, North Korea and Cuba. The former is perhaps the world's most disastrous state, its people on or even past the verge of starvation while its regime develops advanced weaponry. The small island nation of Cuba is the one remaining apparently sustainable communist society. In spite of enormous difficulties—including a counterproductive embargo by the United States and abandonment by its former patron, Russia—it has retained a reasonably egalitarian society and has provided for the basic needs of its people. The Cuban political regime has not, however, permitted democracy, so we do not know whether it retains the support of its people and whether it can survive the transition to a new leader.

Not much is left of the dream, therefore. The dream embodied a great deal of what is best about human aspirations—but it failed. While they lasted, most communist societies thoroughly violated human rights and the norms of justice. Moreover, they did not last. Capitalism is not a transitional phase to a utopian world order. The utopian world order has come and gone.

The Future of Capitalism

The future is unknowable, and we will surely be surprised by what it deals us. Virtually no one in the mid-1950s expected the European empires to disappear within a few years. Virtually no one in the mid-1980s foresaw the collapse of communism and the disintegration of the Soviet Union. Perhaps the world capitalist system will be gone within a few years as well. Such a change is unlikely, however. Capitalism is growing in power, scope, and achievements. It is hard to see any force on the horizon strong enough even to threaten capitalism, let alone overthrow it. The chances are good that we, our children, and our grandchildren will live in a capitalist system. Moreover—and this is a more controversial statement in view of the evident injustices of capitalism—capitalism should not be overthrown. On the whole, our experiences with the dream—and they have been extensive—have been nightmares. There is no exit; we have to learn to manage what we have.

Periodical Bibliography

The following articles have been selected to supplement the diverse views presented in this chapter.

Atlantic Monthly	"Ranking the Rich," September 2004.
Harlan Beckley	"Minding the Gap: Facing Up to Inequalities," *Christian Century*, June 14, 2003.
Andrew Bernstein	"Global Capitalism: Curing Oppression and Poverty," *Freeman*, December 2003.
Jagdish Bhagwati	"Do Multinational Corporations Hurt Poor Countries?" *American Enterprise*, June 2004.
Gregg Easterbrook	"Safe Deposit: The Case for Foreign Aid," *New Republic*, July 29, 2002.
Ed Finn	"Corporate Globalization—Economically, Ecologically Disastrous," *New Catholic Times*, September 7, 2003.
Frances Fukuyama	"The Left Should Love Globalization," *Wall Street Journal*, December 1, 1999.
Sam Ginden	"Social Justice and Globalization: Are They Incompatible?" *Monthly Review*, June 2002.
Robert Guest	"Africa Earned Its Debt," *New York Times*, October 6, 2004.
Tom Hayden	"Seeking a New Globalism in Chiapas: Opponents of the Neoliberal Model Are Demanding a New Social Contract," *Nation*, April 7, 2003.
Jim Lacey	"We're Number Twenty?! The Odd, Anti-American Scorekeeping of the Center for Global Development," *National Review*, June 30, 2003.
Prakash Loungani	"Inequality: Now You See It, Now You Don't," *Finance & Development*, September 2003.
Branko Milanovic	"Inequality in the World Economy—by the Numbers," *Multinational Monitor*, July/August 2003.
Cynthia Moe-Loebeda	"Refuting the False Gospel of Globalization," *The Other Side*, November/December 2002.
New Republic	"March Madness," May 1, 2000.
Jim Peron	"Antiglobalists Are Scarce in Poor Countries," *Freeman*, June 2004.
Robert J. Polack	"Social Justice and the Global Economy: New Challenges for Social Work in the 21st Century," *Social Work*, April 2004.

Andrew Rice   "Letter from Uganda," *Nation*, August 30, 2004.

Peter Singer   "The Singer Solution to World Poverty," *New York Times Magazine*, September 5, 1999.

Michael D. Yates   "Poverty and Inequality in the Global Economy," *Monthly Review*, February 2004.

For Further Discussion

Chapter 1

1. What does Bill Moyers mean when he talks about the "balance between wealth and commonwealth?" After reading his article, do you agree or disagree that concentration of private wealth is in itself harmful to society? Explain.

2. John Kekes disparages "egalitarians" in his viewpoint. Does Bill Moyers, based on his arguments in the first viewpoint, qualify as an egalitarian, as Kekes describes the term? Explain why or why not.

3. Citizens for a Sound Economy consistently refers to the "death tax" while William H. Gates Sr. and Chuck Collins instead refer to the "estate tax." Why might the authors choose one term over the other? How important do you think such nomenclature is in framing the debate over whether this tax should be repealed or retained? Why?

4. Bill Quigley asks two questions that serve as underlying premises to his proposal for a living wage constitutional amendment: whether people who want to work should have that opportunity, and whether people who work full-time should earn enough to be able to support themselves and their families. What is your answer to these questions? How do you believe the other authors in this chapter would answer them? Do you think that answering "yes" to these questions commits you to support a government-mandated minimum wage? Why or why not?

5. Thomas Sowell argues that both "social justice" and "living wage" are attractive-sounding phrases that distort or hide factual realities. Do you agree or disagree with this assertion? Defend your answer, using the viewpoints.

Chapter 2

1. Paul Street argues that many social phenomena in America make sense if viewed through the prism of race. In which of his examples do you find the connection to racism to be the strongest? The weakest?

2. In your opinion, does the example of one person—Oprah Winfrey—constitute a decisive argument against racial oppression in America, as David Horowitz suggests? Why or why not?

3. E.A. Rohrbach Perry cites the story of one family as an example of why affirmative action is necessary. Is her use of a single ex-

ample more or less persuasive than Horowitz's example of Oprah Winfrey? Defend your answer.

4. What do you make of Steven Yates's basketball analogy in his attack on affirmative action programs: Does his analogy accurately depict what affirmative action entails, in your opinion? Why or why not?

5. Steven Yates identifies himself as a white man in his attack on affirmative action. What point do you believe he is attempting to make by such an identification? Do you believe that his race is relevant in critiquing his arguments? Are attacks on affirmative action more credible in your mind if they come from a member of a minority group? Why or why not?

6. Linda Chavez concedes that slavery is an evil and that slaves should have been compensated after the Civil War. Why does she then oppose slavery reparations today? After reading the arguments of Chavez and Manning Marable, do you believe that African Americans should as a matter of justice receive financial compensation? Explain your answer.

Chapter 3

1. Joel Wendland's article is taken from the official publication of the Communist Party USA. How does this affiliation affect your evaluation of his argument?

2. Denise Venable, Rebecca A. Thacker, and Joshua C. Hall all contend that the wage gap between the genders is due to the different education, skills, and lifestyle choices of men and women. What evidence do they provide to back up their argument? Is this argument addressed in the articles by Joel Wendland and Heather Boushey? Who is more convincing, in your view? Why?

3. Joan Kennedy Taylor argues that women should take individual responsibility for learning how to cope in an integrated workplace and that sexual harassment laws and policies prevent this. Equal Rights Advocates contends that harassment laws are necessary to empower women to cope with sexual harassment. After reading the two selections, describe in specific ways how sexual harassment policies both hamper and/or enable women to cope with workplace difficulties.

Chapter 4

1. Kai Nielsen lists a number of statistics about global poverty to argue that global capitalism is unjust. Does he do enough to connect the problems he describes with global capitalism, in your opinion? Why or why not?

2. Johan Norberg argues that globalization has been made a scapegoat—it is blamed for social problems it does not cause. After reading his viewpoint and that of Kai Nielsen, do you agree or disagree with this assessment? Defend your answer, citing from the viewpoints.

3. Jean-Bertrand Aristide has been a controversial figure throughout his political career in Haiti. Some people have hailed him as a hero while others have accused him of being a despot. Do you believe his background as a politician lends greater or lesser credence to the arguments presented in his viewpoint? Why or why not?

4. Doug Bandow and Jean-Bertrand Aristide paint differing pictures of "peasant" life in developing nations. Do you believe people in the United States overly romanticize life in other countries, as Bandow suggests? Explain your answer.

5. Ken Boettcher calls for a socialist revolution; John Isbister argues that socialism has already been tried and has been a failure. Are Isbister's concerns adequately addressed in Boettcher's article, in your opinion? Explain.

6. Does the fact that John Isbister is far more critical of capitalism than Johan Norberg lend greater strength to his ultimate defense of capitalism? Explain why or why not.

Organizations to Contact

The editors have compiled the following list of organizations concerned with the issues debated in this book. The descriptions are derived from materials provided by the organizations. All have publications or information available for interested readers. The list was compiled on the date of publication of the present volume; names, addresses, phone and fax numbers, and e-mail and Internet addresses may change. Be aware that many organizations take several weeks or longer to respond to inquiries, so allow as much time as possible.

African American Jewish Coalition for Justice (AAJCJ)
PO Box 22843, Seattle, WA 98122-0843
e-mail: aajcj@aajcj.org • Web site: www.aajcj.org
The AAJCJ is a group of African and Jewish Americans who have joined in a coalition to fight racial and ethnic discrimination in the United States. The group asserts that slavery reparations will help heal America's racial divide and provide African Americans with more social and economic opportunities. It publishes the monthly online newsletter *Coalition Connection* and posts member articles, such as "Reparations: An Issue of Justice and Much More," on its Web site.

American Association for Affirmative Action
12100 Sunset Hills Rd., Suite 130, Reston, VA 20190
(800) 252-8952 • fax: (703) 435-4390
Web site: www.affirmativeaction.org
The American Association for Affirmative Action is a group of equal opportunity/affirmative action officers concerned with the implementation of affirmative action in employment and in education nationwide. Information on affirmative action programs can be found on its Web site.

American Civil Liberties Union (ACLU)
125 Broad St., Eighteenth Fl., New York, NY 10004
(212) 549-2500 • fax: (212) 549-2646
Web site: www.aclu.org
The ACLU is a national organization that works to defend Americans' civil rights and liberties as guaranteed by the U.S. Constitution. It works to establish equality before the law, regardless of race, color, sexual orientation, or national origin. The ACLU publishes and distributes policy statements, pamphlets, and the semiannual newsletter *Civil Liberties Alert.*

American Friends Service Committee (AFSC)
1501 Cherry St., Philadelphia, PA 19102
(215) 241-7000 • fax: (215) 241-7275
e-mail: afscinfo@afsc.org • Web site: www.afsc.org
The AFSC is a Quaker organization that attempts to relieve human suffering and find new approaches to world peace and social justice through nonviolence. Its publications include the periodical *Quaker Action* and the newsletter *Toward Peace and Justice*. It has also published *Human Rights Report: Voices from the Border*, which is available on its Web site.

Cato Institute
1000 Massachusetts Ave. NW, Washington, DC 20001-5403
(202) 842-0200 • fax: (202) 842-3490
e-mail: cato@cato.org • Web site: www.cato.org
The Cato Institute is a libertarian public policy research foundation dedicated to limiting the control of government and protecting individual liberties. It offers numerous publications on public policy issues, including the triannual *Cato Journal*, the bimonthly newsletter *Cato Policy Report*, and the quarterly magazine *Regulation*.

Center for Economic and Social Justice
PO Box 40711, Washington, DC 20016
(703) 243-5155 • fax: (703) 243-5935
e-mail: thirdway@cesj.org • Web site: www.cesj.org
The Center for Economic and Social Justice is a nonprofit, nonpartisan, ecumenical, all-volunteer organization. It promotes a free enterprise approach to global economic justice through expanded capital ownership. Among its publications are *Toward Economic and Social Justice* and *The Capitalist Manifesto*. Press releases and other materials are available on its Web site.

Center for Equal Opportunity (CEO)
14 Pidgeon Hill Dr., Suite 500, Sterling, VA 20165
(703) 421-5443 • fax: (703) 421-6401
e-mail: comment@ceousa.org • Web site: www.ceousa.org
The Center for Equal Opportunity is a think tank devoted exclusively to the promotion of color-blind equal opportunity and racial harmony. CEO sponsors conferences, supports research, and publishes policy briefs on issues related to race, ethnicity, assimilation, and public policy. *The Tragedy of Civil Rights: How Equal Opportunity Became Equal Results* and *Not a Close Question: Preferences in University Admissions* are among its publications.

Center for the Study of Popular Culture (CSPC)
4401 Wilshire Blvd., Fourth Fl., Los Angeles, CA 90010
Web site: www.cspc.org
Web site: www.frontpagemagazine.com
The CSPC was founded to challenge the radical leftism its members argue is endemic in American universities and media outlets. Its president, David Horowitz, is a leading critic of the slavery reparations movement. The CSPC distributes the book *Uncivil War: The Controversy over Reparations for Slavery*. It also publishes numerous articles on reparations and other issues on its Web site.

Center of Concern
1225 Otis St. NE, Washington, DC 20017
(202) 635-2757 • fax: (202) 832-9494
e-mail: coc@coc.org • Web site: www.coc.org
The Center of Concern engages in social analysis, theological reflection, policy advocacy, and public education on issues of justice and peace. Its programs and writings include subjects such as international development, women's roles, economic alternatives, and a theology based on justice for all peoples. It publishes the bimonthly newsletter *Center Focus* as well as numerous papers and books, including *Opting for the Poor: A Challenge for North Americans*.

Claremont Institute
937 W. Foothill Blvd., Suite E, Claremont, CA 91711
(909) 621-6825 • fax: (909) 626-6824
e-mail: info@claremont.org • Web site: www.claremont.org
The Claremont Institute aims to restore the principles of the American founding in social policies. It supports limited government and opposes affirmative action initiatives. Its publications include *America's Passion for Fairness* and *Equal Opportunity Denied: Nine Case Studies in Reverse Discrimination*.

Economic Policy Institute
1660 L. St. NW, Suite 1200, Washington, DC 20036
(202) 775-8810 • fax: (202) 775-0819
e-mail: epi@epinet.org • Web site: www.epinet.org
The Economic Policy Institute conducts research and promotes education programs on economic policy issues, particularly the economics of poverty, unemployment, and American industry. It supports organized labor and living wage ordinances. It publishes the triannual *Economic Policy Institute Journal*.

Global Exchange

2017 Mission St., #303, San Francisco, CA 94110
(415) 255-7296 • fax: (415) 255-7498
Web site: www.globalexchange.org

Global Exchange is a nonprofit organization that promotes social justice, environmental sustainability, and grassroots activism on international human rights issues. Global Exchange produces various books, videos, and other educational programs and materials concerning human rights.

Independent Women's Forum

1726 M St. NW, Tenth Fl., Washington, DC 20036
(202) 419-1820
e-mail: info@iwf.org • Web site: www.iwf.org

The Independent Women's Forum is a nonprofit, nonpartisan organization founded by women to foster public education and debate about legal, social, and economic policies affecting women and families. It opposes the women-as-victims, pro–big-government ideology of radical feminism. News releases and commentaries on such issues as the gender wage gap are published on its Web site.

Living Wage Resource Center

1486 Dorchester Ave., Boston, MA 02122
(617) 740-9500 • fax: (617) 436-4878
Web site: www.livingwagecampaign.org

The Living Wage Resource Center is a project of the Association of Community Organizations for Reform Now (ACORN), the nation's oldest and largest grassroots organization of low-income people. Its Web site includes a brief history of the national living wage movement, background materials such as ordinance summaries and comparisons, and other materials designed to help activists work for laws mandating a living wage. It also produces the *Living Wage Campaign Organizing Manual.*

National Association for the Advancement of Colored People (NAACP)

4605 Mt. Hope Dr., Baltimore, MD 21215
(877) NAACP-98
Web site: www.naacp.org

The primary focus of the NAACP continues to be the protection and enhancement of the civil rights of African Americans and other minorities. The NAACP works at the national, regional, and local level to secure civil rights through advocacy for supportive legislation and by the implementation of strategic initiatives. The organization publishes *Crisis*, a bimonthly magazine, and provides press releases on its Web site.

National Committee on Pay Equity
1925 K St. NW, Suite 402, Washington, DC 20006-1119
(202) 223-8360, ext. 8 • fax: (202) 776-0537
e-mail: fairpay@patriot.net • Web site: www.pay-equity.org
The National Committee on Pay Equity is a national coalition of labor, women's, and civil rights organizations and individuals working to achieve pay equity by eliminating sex- and race-based wage discrimination. Its publications include a quarterly newsletter, *Newsnotes*, and numerous books and briefing papers on the issue of pay equity.

National Organization for Women (NOW)
733 Fifteenth St. NW, Second Fl., Washington, DC 20005
(202) 628-8669 • fax: (202) 785-8576
e-mail: now@now.org • Web site: www.now.org
The National Organization for Women is the largest organization of feminist activists in the United States. NOW's goal is to take action to bring about equality for all women. NOW works to promote affirmative action and eliminate discrimination and harassment in the workplace, schools, and justice system. The organization offers a quarterly publication, the *National NOW Times*, and publishes occasional reports and white papers.

Reason Public Policy Institute (RPPI)
3415 S. Sepulveda Blvd., Suite 400, Los Angeles, CA 90034
(310) 391-2245 • fax: (310) 391-4395
e-mail: feedback@reason.org • Web site: www.rppi.org
The RPPI is a research organization that supports less government interference in the lives of Americans. It has published critical articles on slavery reparations, affirmative action, and other issues on its Web site and in its monthly magazine, *Reason*.

Rockford Institute
928 N. Main St., Rockford, IL 61103
(815) 964-5053 • fax: (815) 964-9403
e-mail: info@rockfordinstitute.org
Web site: www.chroniclesmagazine.org
The institute is a conservative research center that studies capitalism, religion, and liberty. It has published numerous articles questioning government and legislative solutions to social problems in

its monthly magazine, *Chronicles*, recent issues of which are available on its Web site.

TransAfrica Forum
1426 Twenty-first St. NW, Washington, DC 20036
(202) 223-1960 • fax: (202) 223-1966
e-mail: info@transafricaforum.org
Web site: www.transafricaforum.org

TransAfrica Forum conducts research on U.S. foreign and economic policy and its effect on African peoples in Latin America, the Caribbean, and the African continent. It is a leader in the movement to win slavery reparations for Africans from the U.S. government. It posts reports and papers in support of these efforts on its Web site.

United for a Fair Economy (UFE)
37 Temple Pl., Second Fl., Boston, MA 02111
(617) 423-2148 • fax: (617) 423-0191
Web site: www.faireconomy.org

United for a Fair Economy is a nonpartisan, nonprofit organization that believes that concentrated wealth and power undermine the economy, corrupt democracy, deepen the racial divide, and tear communities apart. It produces books and reports, including *I Didn't Do It Alone: Society's Contribution to Individual Wealth and Success* and provides articles and other references on its Web site to help build social movements for greater equality.

United States Conference of Catholic Bishops (USCCB)
3211 Fourth St. NE, Washington, DC 20017
(202) 541-3000
Web site: www.nccbuscc.org

The USCCB is an organization of the U.S. hierarchy of the Roman Catholic Church that serves to coordinate and promote Catholic activities in the United States and to organize charitable and social welfare work. It issues publications and statements on many social justice issues, including globalization, third world debt relief, hunger, and foreign aid.

Urban Institute
2100 M St. NW, Washington, DC 20037
(202) 261-5244
Web site: www.urban.org

The Urban Institute investigates social and economic problems confronting the nation and analyzes efforts to solve these problems.

In addition, the institute works to improve government decisions and to increase citizen awareness about important public choices. It offers a wide variety of resources, including the report *Discrimination in Metropolitan Housing Markets.*

WorldViews
464 Nineteenth St., Oakland, CA 94612-2297
(510) 451-1742 • fax: (510) 835-3017
e-mail: worldviews@igc.org • Web site: www.worldviews.igc.org

WorldViews gathers, organizes, and publicizes information and educational resource materials that deal with issues of peace and justice in world affairs. It publicizes and promotes the print and audiovisual resources produced by writers, editors, filmmakers, and others around the world who are struggling to build just and peaceful societies. The organization also publishes *WorldViews: A Quarterly Review of Resources for Education and Action* and the *Third World Resource Directory.*

Bibliography of Books

Maurianne Adams et al., eds. — *Readings for Diversity and Social Justice: An Anthology on Racism, Sexism, Anti-Semitism, Heterosexism, Classism, and Ableism.* New York: Routledge, 2000.

William Kweku Asare — *Slavery Reparations in Perspective.* New Bern, NC: Trafford, 2003.

Gerald Beigel — *Faith and Social Justice in the Teaching of Pope John Paul II.* New York: Peter Lang, 1997.

Gilberto Cárdenas, ed. — *La Causa: Civil Rights, Social Justice, and the Struggle for Equality in the Midwest.* Houston, TX: Arte Público Press, 2004.

Matt Cavanagh — *Against Equality of Opportunity.* New York: Clarendon Press, 2002.

Michel Chossudovsky — *The Globalisation of Poverty: Impacts of IMF and World Bank Reforms.* Mapusa, Goa, India: Other India Press, 2001.

Lee Cokorinos — *The Assault on Diversity: An Organized Challenge to Racial and Gender Justice.* Lanham, MD: Rowman & Littlefield, 2003.

Giovanni Andrea Cornia, ed. — *Inequality, Growth, and Poverty in an Era of Liberalization and Globalization.* New York: Oxford University Press, 2004.

Pablo de Greiff and Ciaran Cronin, eds. — *Global Justice and Transnational Politics; Essays on the Moral and Political Challenges of Globalization.* Cambridge, MA: MIT Press, 2002.

Keith Dowding et al., eds. — *The Ethics of Stakeholding.* New York: Palgrave Macmillan, 2003.

Joe R. Feagin — *Racist America: Roots, Current Realities, and Future Reparations.* New York: Routledge, 2000.

Ellen Frank — *The Raw Deal: How Myths and Misinformation About Deficits, Inflation, and Wealth Impoverish America.* Boston: Beacon Press, 2004.

Stephan Gilliatt — *How the Poor Adapt to Poverty in Capitalism.* Lewiston, NY: Edwin Mellen Press, 2001.

Patrick Hayden — *John Rawls: Towards a Just World Order.* Cardiff: University of Wales Press, 2002.

David Horowitz — *Uncivil Wars: The Controversy over Reparations for Slavery.* San Francisco: Encounter Books, 2002.

John P. Jackson · *Social Scientists for Social Justice: Making the Case Against Segregation.* New York: New York University Press, 2001.

Timothy P. Jackson · *The Priority of Love: Christian Charity and Social Justice.* Princeton, NJ: Princeton University Press, 2003.

Mohammad Hashim Kamali · *Freedom, Equality, and Justice in Islam.* Cambridge: Islamic Texts Society, 2002.

Michael S. Kimmel · *The Gendered Society.* New York: Oxford University Press, 2004.

Michael S. Kimmel and Amy Aronson, eds. · *The Gendered Society Reader.* New York: Oxford University Press, 2004.

Mary C. King, ed. · *Squaring Up: Policy Strategies to Raise Women's Incomes in the United States.* Ann Arbor: University of Michigan Press, 2001.

Christopher Lake · *Equality and Responsibility.* New York: Oxford University Press, 2001.

Timothy Macklem · *Beyond Comparison: Sex and Discrimination.* New York: Cambridge University Press, 2003.

Deepa Narayan, ed. · *Can Anyone Hear Us?* New York: Oxford University Press, 2000.

Vicente Navarro, ed. · *The Political Economy of Social Inequalities.* Amityville, NY: Baywood, 2000.

Robert L. Nelson and William P. Bridges · *Legalizing Gender Inequality: Courts, Markets, and Unequal Pay for Women in America.* New York: Cambridge University Press, 1999.

David Neumark · *Sex Differences in Labor Markets.* New York: Routledge, 2004.

Otto Newman and Richard de Zoysa · *The Promise of the Third Way; Globalization and Social Justice.* New York: Palgrave, 2001.

Martha C. Nussbaum · *Sex and Social Justice.* New York: Oxford University Press, 1999.

Fred L. Pincus · *Reverse Discrimination: Dismantling the Myth.* Boulder, CO: Lynne Rienner, 2003.

Thomas W. Pogge, ed. · *Global Justice.* Malden, MA: Blackwell, 2001.

Randall Robinson · *The Debt: What America Owes to Blacks.* New York: Dutton, 2000.

Stephen Steinberg · *Turning Back: The Retreat from Racial Justice in American Thought and Policy.* Boston: Beacon Press, 2001.

Anthony Stith   *Breaking the Glass Ceiling: Sexism and Racism in Corporate America.* Toronto, Canada: Warwick, 1998.

Richard F. Tomasson   *Affirmative Action: The Pros and Cons of Policy and Practice.* Lanham, MD: Rowman & Little-field, 2001.
et al.

Sarah Owen Vandersluis   *Poverty in World Politics: Whose Global Era?* New
and Paris Yeros, eds.   York: St. Martin's Press, 2000.

Raymond A.   *Should America Pay? Slavery and the Raging
Winbush, ed.   Debate on Reparations.* New York: Amistad, 2003.

Index

183

184